Two Plays for Young People
Fairytaleheart and *Sparkleshark*

Philip Ridley was born in the East End of London, where he still lives and works. He studied painting at St Martin's School of Art and has exhibited throughout Europe, New York and Japan. As a writer his credits include three adult novels, *Crocodilia* (1988), *In the Eyes of Mr Fury* (1989) and *Flamingoes in Orbit* (1990); three plays for radio, *October Scars the Skin* (1989), *The Aquarium of Coincidences* (1989) and *Shambolic Rainbow* (1991); seven children's novels, *Mercedes Ice* (1989), *Dakota of the White Flats* (1989), *Krindlekrax* (1991), winner of the Smarties Prize for Children's Fiction and the W. H. Smith Mind-Boggling Books Award, *Meteorite Spoon* (1994), *Kaspar in the Glitter* (1994), shortlisted for the Whitbread Best Children's Novel Award, *Scribbleboy* (1997), which received a commendation at the Nasen Special Education Needs Book Awards, and *ZinderZunder* (1998); and two pieces for younger children, *The Hooligan's Shampoo* (1995) and *Dreamboat Zing* (1996). His stage plays are *The Pitchfork Disney* (1991), *The Fastest Clock in the Universe* (1992), which won the Meyer-Whitworth Prize, a *Time Out* Award, and both the Critics' Circle and the *Evening Standard* Theatre Awards for Most Promising Playwright, *Ghost from a Perfect Place* (1994), and two plays for young people, *Sparkleshark* (Royal National Theatre, 1997) and *Fairytaleheart* (Hampstead Theatre, 1998). His short film, *The Universe of Dermot Finn* (1988), was followed by his screenplay for *The Krays* (1990), winner of the *Evening Standard* British Film of the Year Award, and his début feature film as both writer and director, the cult classic *The Reflecting Skin* (1990), which won eleven international awards and was voted one of the Best Ten Films of 1991 by the *Los Angeles Times*. In 1991 he was awarded the Most Promising Newcomer to British Film at the *Evening Standard* Film Awards. His second feature film as both writer and director, *The Passion of Darkly Noon* (1995), won the Best Director at the Porto Film Festival. His work has been translated into sixteen languages.

PHILIP RIDLEY

Plays for Young People

Fairytaleheart
and
Sparkleshark

faber and faber

First published in 1998
by Faber and Faber Limited
3 Queen Square London WC1N 3AU

Photoset by Parker Typesetting Service, Leicester
Printed in England by Mackays of Chatham plc, Chatham, Kent

A CIP record for this book
is available from the British Library
ISBN 0-571-19624-1

2 4 6 8 10 9 7 5 3 1

Contents

FAIRYTALEHEART

For all the Gideons
of the World

'Nothing matters but faith
to what matters inside the heart.
Write that down for a start.'
George Macbeth

Characters

Kirsty
Gideon

Fairytaleheart was first performed at Hampstead Theatre, London, on 27 January 1998 with the following cast:

Gideon Zoot Lynam
Kirsty Victoria Shalet

Director Philip Ridley
Designer Jessica Stack
Lighting Tim Mitchell
Sound John A. Leonard
Dialect Coach Barbara Houseman

The stage of an abandoned community centre in the East End of London. Most of the windows are broken and boarded over (concealing the snowy, March evening outside) so what is about to be described is, for the moment, barely discernible.

There's a couple of old chairs, several boxes, a table and various scattered detritus. The table is covered with painting materials: brushes, tubes of paint, spray paint, whatever is needed to have created –

The fairytale backdrop. This covers most of stage and has been created by adapting and painting found objects: a pile of boxes has become a mountain; an old mantelpiece, a cave; a sheet of corrugated iron, a river; a large mirrorball, a sun or moon. Also depicted are birds, flowers and butterflies.

Some distance from the main backdrop – and lying flat on the ground – is a large mirror. Flowers have been painted round it, giving the impression of a pond.

The general effect is of a magical landscape, somewhere between a painting and sculpture. The magical quality will eventually intensify by the shimmering light of –

Candles. These are everywhere on stage: across the floor, on table. Candles of all shapes and sizes. Most are in coloured-glass containers. They are, of course, unlit at present.

Pause.

Then –

The entrance at the back of the auditorium noisily unlocks and –

Kirsty enters. She is fifteen years old and carrying a bag of hastily packed clothes in one hand and a torch in the other. She is shivering against the cold outside. Hardly surprising considering her clothing – obviously her 'party best': a dress decorated with silver sequins and rhinestones, silver stilettos and a short, white, fake-fur coat. Her hair is neatly styled and highlighted with silver glitter. She's tried hard to make an impression and succeeded.

Kirsty closes the door behind her and switches on the torch. The beam of light pokes through the darkness like a luminous finger.

Kirsty Hello?

Slight pause.

Anyone there?

Kirsty walks through the auditorium and up onto stage. She seems familiar with the community hall as a whole, but not the paints and backdrop, etc. She treads carefully round the candles, then shines torch over backdrop.
Pause.

She puts bag down, then – a little awkwardly – picks up a brush, dips it into some paint, and adds some colour to one of the butterflies.

Pause.

Then –

The entrance at the back of the auditorium noisily unlocks and –

Gideon enters. He is fifteen years old and carrying a well-worn duffel bag in one hand and a torch in the other. His hair is longish and aspires to be dreadlocks. He is well insulated against the cold: a thick and baggy (albeit worn) jumper, a couple of coats, scarf, gloves and paint-splattered boots. Nothing really goes together but – on him – it works.

Kirsty turns torch off and puts brush down.

Gideon Who . . . who's there?

Closes door and fumbles to light torch.

Who are you?

Kirsty Don't panic.

Gideon I don't mean you any harm.

Kirsty Don't mean me any – What are you prattling on about?

Turns on her torch.

I said, Don't panic.

Gideon turns on his torch and approaches stage.

Gideon . . . You're Kirsty.

Kirsty How d'you know my bloody name?

Gideon Must have heard it around.

Kirsty *(flinching at torchlight)* Do you mind?

Gideon *(aiming torch away)* Sorry.

Gets on stage.
Slight pause.

You live in the block of flats by the playground, don't you?

Kirsty If you call a sandpit full of dogs' poo a playground, then, yes, that's where I live. Heard that around too, did you?

Gideon Must have.

Kirsty You'll be telling me my flat number next.

Gideon Thirteen.

Kirsty You been spying on me?

Gideon No.

Starts removing coats, gloves and scarf.

Unlucky for some, eh?

Kirsty . . . What?

Gideon Thirteen.

Kirsty I'm not superstitious.

Slight pause.

Gideon How did you get in?

Kirsty I unlocked the door.

Gideon With what?

Kirsty A pilchard with rigor mortis – What do you think I unlocked it with? A key!

Gideon The only key belongs to me.

Kirsty Correction. It belongs to your Dad. Who's the caretaker of the estate. And, as this is the community hall of said estate – or, it *was* – then the key is . . . blah, blah, blah.

Slight pause.

Gideon You been spying on me?

Kirsty It's a small estate.

Pause.

Gideon So where did you get your key from?

Kirsty You get a degree in being nosy or something? Spanish Inquisition'd give me an easier bloody time.

Gideon Don't tell me if you don't want to.

Slight pause.

Kirsty It's my Mum's, if you must know.

Gideon Your Mum died, didn't she?

Kirsty You asking me or telling me?

Slight pause.

Yes, she died. Two years ago. Two years and seven months.

Slight pause.

Before she got sick she used to help out here. Help out – what am I saying? She *ran* it. When it really was a community centre. When the windows weren't boarded up. When people used to come to have tea and gossip. Or play bingo. Disco for kids. Mum knew everyone's name. This was her . . . her . . .

Gideon Her kingdom.

Slight pause.

Kirsty It was.

Gideon I've heard people on the estate talk about her. She was real popular, your Mum. Beautiful too, they say.

Slight pause.

Kirsty Bloody hell, it's like a fridge in here.

Gideon There's no electric.

Kirsty I know.

Gideon Then you should have dressed properly.

Kirsty I am dressed properly. I'm just not dressed . . . suitably.

Gideon You're welcome to one of my coats.

Kirsty . . . They look a bit damp.

Gideon My jumper then. It's warm with body heat.

Kirsty . . . I'd rather not.

Gideon But your lips are blue.

Kirsty Must be the lipstick.

Gideon Blue tights too, eh?

Kirsty You leave my tights out of this.

Gideon I'm wearing thermal pants.

Kirsty Thank you for sharing that with me – If you keep shining it in my eyes I'll thump you.

Gideon You're shining yours.

Slight pause.
　Slowly, they avert torchlight from each other's face.

Gideon It's snowing outside.

Kirsty So that's what that white stuff's called.

Gideon Ain't you got any thermal knickers?

Kirsty glares and gasps.
　Slight pause.
　Gideon takes flask from his duffel bag.

Gideon You want something warm to drink?

Kirsty No, thank you.

Gideon It's peppermint tea with a drop of lavender oil.

Kirsty That's supposed to tempt me?

Gideon Lavender helps you relax.

Kirsty I am bloody relaxed!

Gideon pours himself a drink from flask. He takes a few noisy slurps.
Kirsty glances at him, irritated.
Slight pause.
Gideon takes a sandwich, wrapped in silver foil, from his duffel bag.

Gideon Something to eat?

Kirsty I dread to ask. What is it?

Gideon Tofu and pine nut sandwich.

Kirsty Bloody hell! Ain't you got anything as basic as crisps and a Coke?

Gideon Not on me, no.

Kirsty I'm not hungry.

Gideon takes a bite from the sandwich. He eats as noisily as he drinks.
Kirsty's irritation increases. Until –

Kirsty Must you?

Gideon What?

Kirsty Eat . . . like that!

Gideon Like what?

Slight pause.

I'll save the rest for later.

Puts sandwich and flask back in duffel bag.

Gideon The cold does amazing things! Don't you think?

Slight pause.

On the way here the snot up my nose froze. It was funny –
I sneezed and this rock hard bogey shot out. Lethal it was.
Like a bullet.

Kirsty Killed by a frozen bogey. The cherry on the cake of
my day.

Pause.

Gideon Snow makes everything look beautiful.

Kirsty Take more than snow to make this dump of an
estate beautiful.

Gideon You're wrong . . . Snow falling in the night sky.
Like . . . like twinkling bits of . . . starlight. There! How's
that? And as it falls it changes colour. The street lights, you
see – They turn the snow orange and yellow. Like burning
feathers. Yes! It settles. The grey concrete – it's gone. The
cracked pavement – gone. Supermarket trolleys – gone.
Piles of rubbish – gone. In their place? A twinkling
wonderland. When you walk – crunch, crunch, crunch.
Apart from that – silence.

Slight pause.

Your eyes look a bit bloodshot.

Kirsty . . . It's the cold. Makes my eyes water.

Gideon Wanna handkerchief?

Takes handkerchief from pocket.

Kirsty Ugh! No! I've got a clean one thank you.

*Rummages in her bag. Unable to find handkerchief, she
uses a T-shirt.*
Slight pause.

Gideon You going to the launderette?

Kirsty Launder –? Oh, no.

Slight pause.

Gideon (*indicating her coat*) Hope that's not real fur.

Kirsty This? Baby seal. Culled it myself – Of course it's not real fur! What do you think of me?

Slight pause.

Gideon I'll light the candles. That'll warm things up. Mind over matter and all that.

Starts to light candles.

Kirsty I've never seen so many.

Gideon Every time I come I bring a few more. Some are amazing. Look at this one. Got gold bits in it.

Kirsty . . . Why?

Gideon Makes it look nice.

Kirsty Don't see the point. Candle's a candle. All that's important is the flame.

Slight pause.

What's that smell?

Gideon Some of them are aromatic.

Kirsty Harry – what?

Gideon Smell of roses.

Holds candle out for Kirsty to smell.

Kirsty Gold! Roses! They'll be tap-dancing and cooking you pizza next.

Gideon You've got bits in your hair.

Kirsty . . . What?

Gideon Sparkling bits.

Kirsty Oh, that's the hair gel. It's special. Got glitter in it. What did you think it was? Metallic dandruff?

Gideon No, I didn't think that.

Slight pause.

Kirsty Well, I dread to think what's in your hair. When was the last time you washed it?

Gideon Hair don't need washing. It cleans itself. The body's natural oils keep it healthy. Have a feel.

Kirsty You keep your natural oils to yourself.

Gideon Don't you like the style?

Kirsty Oh, it's a *style*, is it?

Gideon Dreadlocks – well, almost, sort of.

Kirsty Dirty rat's tails – well, totally, definitely.

Slight pause.

Gideon My name's Gideon.

Kirsty I know.

Gideon How?

Kirsty I . . . Oh, don't start all that again. As I said, small estate. New face. 'Who's that?' 'Oh, that's the new caretaker's son. His name's Gideon.' All there is to it.

Pause.

Gideon The caretaker's not my Dad.

Kirsty What?

Gideon My real Dad left me and Mum years ago. I was a baby. Never seen him since. Or heard from him. Can't remember what he looks like or anything. Mum had a photograph once – but she burnt it. Don't blame her. I'd

have done the same if someone said, 'I love you', one day,
then packed their bags and cleared off the next, without so
much as a 'Take care of yourself'. So it was just me and
Mum. Until she met this bloke. A few months ago. Love at
first sight or some such thing. Mum just looked at him and
. . . pow! She sort of . . . changed. You know? Like before
. . . we agreed on everything, me and Mum. We'd giggle
and stuff. Now she giggles with him and . . . Don't mind!
Me! Not a bit. Anyway! Where was I . . .? Yes! That's it!
This bloke was just about to start a new job. Caretaker.
Here. So . . . well, blah, blah, blah as you'd say.

Pause.
Kirsty takes unlit candle from table and approaches
Gideon.

Kirsty Let me help.

Gideon Sorry?

Kirsty The candles.

Gideon lights Kirsty's candle.
She starts lighting other candles.
Slight pause.

Kirsty Where were you living before? When it was just
you and your Mum?

Gideon Oh, lots of places. Couple of squats. Didn't like
those much. Toilets didn't work. We had to do everything
in a bucket then throw the gunk down the drain in the
street. Sometimes the big bits wouldn't go down and we
had to –

Kirsty I think I can guess the rest.

Slight pause.

Gideon Lived next to a warehouse once. Every Saturday
night they'd have a rave. Ever been to one?

Kirsty . . . No.

Gideon Music's so loud. Deafening. Used to make my bed shake. Real poltergeist stuff. Amazing.

Kirsty Didn't you complain?

Gideon Why? Only people dancing.

Kirsty Must have kept you awake, though.

Gideon Sleep through anything, me. You like dancing?

Takes small ghetto blaster from duffel bag.

Got some amazing music here!

Kirsty I'm not into music.

Gideon How can you not be into music? It's like saying, 'I'm not into picking my nose.'

Kirsty Well, I'm not into picking my nose either.

Gideon No, but you do it. Being into it or not's got nothing to do with it. You just do it. Same with music.

Kirsty Music and snot. Why have I never seen the connection before?

Slight pause.

Gideon Last place we lived was under a flyover. Nothing but traffic all night. I slept through a car crash once. Police sirens, ambulance, everything.

Kirsty How come?

Gideon Told you, sleep through anything, me.

Kirsty No – How come you were living under a flyover?

Gideon Oh, we were in a caravan. Staying with some friends of Mum's.

Kirsty Gypsies?

Gideon Not really. Just . . . well, just travellers, I guess. Gave me and Mum a caravan to ourselves. They let me paint it. I put shooting stars and comets and rainbows all over. Looked amazing. At night we'd sit round a little campfire. Mum'd tell stories. She tells the most amazing things my Mum. I loved that place. It was right by the canal too. I love the sound of running water, don't you?

Kirsty We've got a leaking toilet at the moment so the charm's lost on me.

Gideon I remember one night. Lying in Mum's arms. By the campfire. Everything a flickering gold. And . . . oh, as I lay there, the sound of the traffic seemed to change. Wasn't traffic any more. It was tropical insects. Jungle sounds. And I imagined the concrete pillars of the flyover were gigantic treetrunks. And the canal was a vast river. Like the Nile or something. Full of crocodiles and hippos. And I imagined all the exotic birds asleep in the undergrowth. Flamingoes, cockatoos, parrots. And the insects. Beautiful, glittering things. Butterflies with wings all colours of the rainbow. And then . . . then I actually felt something gently touch my fingertips. Guess what it was?

Kirsty . . . A butterfly?

Gideon A rat!

Kirsty No!

Gideon The biggest, ugliest, slimiest rat you've ever seen. Big, pink tail. Yellow teeth. It'd crawled out of the canal and was nibbling at my thumbnail.

Kirsty Hope you killed it.

Gideon Why? Wasn't hurting anyone.

Slight pause.

Kirsty Bet your Mum was glad to get out of that caravan and come here.

Gideon She was in love. She'd have gone anywhere and been happy.

Kirsty But . . . how did you feel?

Gideon Oh, live anywhere, me. Squat, warehouse, council flat –

Kirsty No – Your Mum being with this new bloke. Didn't it bother you at all?

Gideon I'm glad Mum's happy.

Kirsty That's not what I asked.

Slight pause.

Gideon Turn your torch off!

Kirsty What? Oh, yes.

They both turn their torches off. All the candles are lit now.

Gideon Magic or what?

Kirsty and Gideon look at the candlelit space.

Kirsty It does feel a bit warmer.

Gideon Sweltering, me.

He removes jumper to reveal a skimpy T-shirt underneath. Kirsty looks at him.
Slight pause.

Gideon What's wrong?

Kirsty Oh – there's a hole in your shirt.

Gideon One in my jeans too.

Bends over to reveal hole near his backside.

Good for ventilation. When I fart it –

Kirsty That's quite enough, thank you.

Gideon takes some painting materials over to mirror on floor and starts mixing paint.

Kirsty You haven't spoken to many girls, have you?

Gideon What?

Kirsty Girls!

Gideon Girls! Oh . . . sure! Zillions of times!

Pause.

Kirsty What you doing?

Gideon Mixing paint.

Kirsty No! Here! All this!

Slight pause.

Gideon A few weeks ago, when I first got here, I thought the whole estate was . . . well, amazing. Honestly. And Mum's boyfriend – he had the keys to everything! One key . . . one key let me into vast underground chambers. Where boilers vibrated and buzzed. Like . . . sleeping giants. Yes! That's it! Another key took me to the highest roof I'd ever been on. The view goes on for miles. At night the city lights up like a . . . a billion flickering candles. All different colours. Another key –

Kirsty Let you in here.

Slight pause.

Gideon It felt so . . . so safe and comfortable. You know!

Warm with all the people who'd used this place. To drink tea and gossip. Bingo. Disco.

Kirsty . . . You felt that?

Slight pause.

Gideon So I asked Mum's boyfriend if I could have the only key – the only *other* key.

Kirsty And you started to come here?

Gideon Every evening.

Kirsty Eight o'clock.

Gideon On the dot. Not that you've been spying, of course.

Slight pause.

Kirsty And you're . . . painting this – what?

Pause.

Gideon Just think of this: all the rubbish taken out. Windows mended. Walls given a lick of paint. Something bright and cheerful. Floor, swept and polished. Perhaps a carpet. Above, lights – oh, yeah, the electrics back on. And up here, on the stage . . . we're doing a play or something. And out there . . .

Indicates audience.

The audience! I can imagine them. Their faces. See them almost. Can you?

Kirsty . . . No.

Gideon You're not trying hard enough.

Kirsty looks out into audience with Gideon.

Gideon They're out there!

Pause.

Hear them?

Kirsty . . . No.

Gideon Concentrate.

Kirsty I am. And I can't.

Gideon I'm sure if you try –

Kirsty Don't push it!

Slight pause.

Gideon What . . . what was I saying? The audience. One day they'll . . . they'll be out there for real. A theatre. That's it. Amazing, eh?

Pause.

Kirsty You're bonkers.

Gideon I . . . I believe if you . . . if you show people something interesting then they'll take an interest.

Kirsty Who said that? Your Mum?

Gideon What if she did?

Kirsty Listen. If you show people round here something interesting, they'll steal it. That's if it *was* interesting in the first place. Which all this, believe me, ain't.

Gideon But . . . but people . . . people –

Kirsty You don't know the first thing about people. You know what people want? What they *really* want? TV. Betting shop. Flash car. Pub. Video and takeaway curry on Saturday night –

Gideon But . . . but I want to give them something else too.

Kirsty What? A bunch of poncey actors.

Gideon No, no. We can do our own stuff. Write it, act it. Me, you, my Mum, your Dad –

Kirsty My Dad! Ha!

Gideon Please don't 'Ha!' Please.

Slight pause.

Let me . . . try to explain.

Slight pause.

Kirsty It's all yours.

Pause.

Well?

Gideon I'm trying to remember – Yes! Got it.

Slight pause.

Imagine this: you're a member of a tribe in the middle of a jungle –

Kirsty I'm what?

Gideon Give me a chance.

Slight pause.

You're a member of a tribe in the middle of a jungle. The date – it has no meaning for you. Why? Because things have remained the same for millenniums. Since the beginning of time. And for you – for you in particular – all your life has been the same. You live with your Dad. In that mud hut over there. See it? Since your Mum died you look after your Dad. You fetch water from the nearby spring. You fish in the river. Your Dad's everything. See the hut yet?

Kirsty . . . Yes.

Gideon And then . . . a scream! Out in the jungle.

Kirsty What is it?

Gideon Someone's been killed.

Kirsty Who?

Gideon A member of the tribe.

Kirsty How?

Gideon There's a monster in the jungle. Some hideous thing. Claws. Teeth.

Kirsty Perhaps a Giant Rat, eh?

Gideon Very likely. And this Giant Rat is knocking off members of your tribe one by one. At night you tremble in fear as the Giant Rat howls and roars. What d'you think we should do?

Kirsty We've got to kill it.

Gideon You and the rest of your tribe get together. You arm yourself with sharpened lengths of bamboo –

Kirsty Is that all?

Gideon 'Fraid so. You scared?

Kirsty A little.

Gideon But you've got to go.

Kirsty Don't know if I can.

Gideon Aha! So that night the Witchdoctor sits the tribe round a fire. The Witchdoctor gives everyone a . . . a relaxing drink made from the pusy boils of giant frogs.

Hands her imaginary drink.

Have a sip.

Kirsty The pusy boils of giant frogs?

Gideon And a few worms.

Slowly, Kirsty drinks.

Gideon And, as the pus 'n' worm mixture takes effect, the Witchdoctor says, 'You're a member of a tribe in the middle of a jungle. Your tribe is being threatened by the terrible Giant Rat. It must be killed. I know you are afraid. But you must face this fear . . .

Slight pause.

The next morning you sharpen your bamboo and go out into the jungle. In the distance you can hear the Giant Rat's massive pink tail slither through the undergrowth. You say, 'In my dreams I have already faced the Giant Rat. I am not afraid.'

Pause.

Kirsty . . . And?

Gideon There is no 'and'.

Kirsty You mean . . . that's it?

Gideon Yes.

Kirsty And you think that explains something?

Gideon . . . Doesn't it?

Kirsty You've been reading too many books.

Gideon It's supposed to explain . . . supposed to . . .

Kirsty Listen, I don't know what orbit you're in, but tell me when the shuttle lands and we might actually have a conversation –

Gideon You listen! You live on an estate. An estate full of cracked concrete. Graffiti. Ruined community centres. You know the date very well. It's one of the millions of facts that fill your mind. You get these facts from computers. Television. Newspapers. Faxes. Internet. You do not believe in Giant Rats. And yet – you're afraid. You don't know why. But something scares you. Oh, it doesn't have sharp teeth or claws or a gigantic, pink tail. But still you're so, so afraid. The fear makes you feel so alone. Makes you cry. Makes you want to run away.

Long pause.
Gideon starts mixing paints again.
Kirsty watches him for a while. Then, slowly, she goes to him.

Kirsty I like that colour.

Gideon Hmm.

Slight pause.

Kirsty It's very bright.

Gideon Hmm.

Slight pause.

Kirsty Like sunshine.

Gideon . . . It's called cadmium yellow.

Kirsty What's that one?

Gideon Monestial blue. Amazing names, eh? Like magic spells. Crimson lake. Rose madder. Lemon yellow.

Kirsty Eye of newt.

Gideon Toe of frog.

Goes to start painting, then –

Hey! I've just realized! It was you!

Kirsty Me what?

Gideon Who painted the butterflies.

Kirsty Oh . . . yes. Couple of nights ago. I couldn't resist.

Gideon Did my head in that.

Kirsty I cleaned the brushes afterwards.

Gideon I thought, What a considerate ghost.

Kirsty You thought I was a ghost.

Gideon Was hoping you were. Making contact with a ghost. Amazing.

Kirsty Scary, you mean.

Gideon What's to be scared of? Ghost's just a lost spirit. Someone who don't believe they're dead. I was gonna help it. Bring a ouija board or something. Tell it, 'Sorry, old son, you've kicked the bucket. Time to move on' – What I thought you were tonight. When I came in.

Kirsty That's why you called, 'I mean you no harm,' like that.

Gideon Got all excited, me.

Kirsty Sorry to disappoint you.

Gideon Oh, you're more interesting than a ghost.

Pause.

Why don't you help me?

Kirsty I'd . . . I'd ruin it.

Gideon Your butterflies are perfect.

Kirsty More interesting than a ghost and perfect butterflies. Certainly is my night for flattery.

Gideon holds out brush and paint.
   Slight pause.
   Slowly, Kirsty takes brush and paint. She goes over to backdrop, hesitates, then removes her coat and lays it carefully on top of her bag. She picks up brush and paint once more.

Kirsty What shall I do?

Gideon Paint some flowers over there.

Kirsty Where? Just here?

Gideon No. That's the cave.

Kirsty Oh, I see. The cave.

Gideon Over there! That's it! There!

   Slight pause.

He doesn't like flowers, you see.

Kirsty Who?

Gideon The Wizard?

Kirsty What Wizard?

Gideon That one there!

Kirsty . . . I don't see him.

Gideon He's in the Magic Cave.

Kirsty Silly me.

   Slight pause.
      Kirsty goes to paint, then hesitates.

Gideon Here! Practise on this first.

   He puts sheet of paper in front of Kirsty.
      Kirsty still hesitates.

31

Gideon Just relax. Imagine soaking in a hot bath. Then think, Flowers! Then let the thought travel out of your head and down your arm. Like an electric current. Buzz. Then out! Splat! Paint it!

Kirsty . . . Relax. Think. Buzz. Splat. Paint.

Gideon All there is to it.

Kirsty closes her eyes.

Gideon That's it. Relax . . . Think, Flowers . . . Let it build up . . . Feel it . . . Feel it . . .

Kirsty starts to tremble.

Gideon Electric current . . . buzzing . . . buzzing . . .

Kirsty trembles some more.

Gideon Now let it travel down your arm . . . That's it . . . Build it up . . . That's it . . . Now – Splat!

With an ecstatic cry, Kirsty starts painting.

Gideon See? Easy?

Kirsty How will I know if I'm doing it right?

Gideon Oh, you'll know. It's like kissing. Sometimes you're smooching away and you're thinking, My nose is in the way! My teeth are too big! Where do I put my hands? That's a wrong kiss. But when it's going right . . . Oh, I bet everything falls into place. No worries. Just an amazing – You *have* been kissed, ain't you?

Kirsty . . . Kissed! Me? Zillions of times!

Slight pause.
    Kirsty continues painting.
    Gideon resumes his own painting.

Kirsty Wh . . . what's the play going to be about?

Gideon No idea yet.

Kirsty You must have.

Gideon Why? Oh, the backdrop! Well, that's just the basics. When Mum makes up her stories they always have a King, Queen, Prince, Princess, Castle, Forest –

Kirsty Wizard?

Gideon Exactly!

Kirsty Fairytales?

Gideon Oh, more than that. The stories are a way of helping me . . . you know, with all the moving and new faces and stuff. Mum says it's just a way of expressing what's really in your heart. Your fairytaleheart, she calls it.

Kirsty Fairytaleheart?

Gideon Amazing, eh? You see, if Mum told me a story about . . . well, a Prince who was misunderstood by everyone except the Queen. Then I'd know that the Queen was my Mum and . . . well – You've got some paint on your skirt.

Kirsty Oh, no! It's brand new.

Gideon I've got something to get it off.

Gets some rags, etc.

Sit down.

Kirsty sits on chair.
Gideon kneels in front of her and starts dabbing paint from skirt.
Slight pause.

Gideon Looks like you.

Kirsty . . . What?

Gideon The flower.

Kirsty How can a flower look like someone?

Gideon It's got your . . . your spirit.

Pause.

Kirsty It's my birthday today.

Gideon Aries! That explains it!

Kirsty I don't believe in horoscopes.

Slight pause.

What're Aries like anyway?

Gideon Fiery. Dominating. Argumentative.

Kirsty I'm not bloody argumentative.

Gideon Many happy returns.

Slight pause.

Kirsty Dad organized a birthday party for me. Back at our flat. Why I'm in this outfit. Had my hair done special too.

Slight pause.

Do you like it?

Gideon Not sure about the metallic dandruff.

Kirsty Lie! Okay? It's called being nice to someone. I fish for a compliment. You give one. Got it?

Gideon . . . Try again.

Kirsty Do you like my hair?

Gideon It's amazing!

Kirsty Thank you.

Slight pause.

34

I ran out of the party. It was horrible.

Gideon Life's too short for horrible parties.

Indicates clean dress.

There! Good as new.

He resumes painting.
Slight pause.

Kirsty Ever since Mum died . . . it's just been me and Dad.
We did everything together. Not that we did much . . . Oh,
I don't want to talk about it.

Gideon had stopped painting to listen.
Now he resumes painting, absently humming.
Slight pause.

Kirsty Some people must have thought it boring. Going to
the pictures with your Dad. Not me. I loved it . . . Oh, I
don't want to talk about it.

Gideon had stopped painting to listen.
Now he resumes painting and humming.
Slight pause.

Kirsty Then one day, we go into the supermarket. Dad's
pushing the trolley. I'm putting things in. Same as usual.
And, suddenly, I turn round – the trolley's gone! 'Dad!' Up
and down the aisles. 'Dad!' There he is! At the checkout.
Talking to . . . someone. Never seen before. Some woman!
Don't like the look of her. Hair styled by a lawnmower.
Colour out of a bottle. Eyelashes fluttering so much it's a
wonder they don't issue a gale warning. And her tits! Talk
about padded bra. You could land a helicopter on them.
And Dad! Look at him! Lapping it up . . . Oh, I don't want
to talk about it! Hear me? I don't want to talk about it!

Gideon had stopped painting to listen.
Now he resumes painting and humming.

Kirsty Ain't you interested?

Gideon You don't want to talk about it.

Kirsty Don't be so obliging! Ask me something.

Slight pause.

Gideon Do you think I should grow a goatee?

Kirsty . . . What?

Gideon A little beard. Just on my chin. I'm sure I've got enough whiskers. Feel?

Kirsty I'm not bothered about that!

Gideon But you said ask you something.

Kirsty Not about bloody whiskers! About . . . her! That woman. Dad's floozie. Say something about her!

Slight pause.

Gideon I think she's nice.

Kirsty You . . . you don't know her.

Gideon I know who you mean. Seen her in the supermarket. She wears a ribbon in her hair.

Kirsty Mutton dressed as lamb!

Gideon Good figure.

Kirsty Deformed!

Gideon Always smiling.

Kirsty Demented!

Gideon Jolly!

Kirsty Oh, yes, she's jolly all right. Got Dad right round her little bloody finger. Like a couple of schoolkids, they are. You should have seen them. At my party too!

Canoodling. Nibbling each other's ears! Disgusting! And every time she looks at my Dad she clutches her chest and goes, 'Ooo! You make my heart go boom-diddy, boom-diddy.'

Gideon Boom-diddy, boom-diddy?

Kirsty Boom-diddy, boom-diddy! Yuk! I tell you, if her brains were dynamite, they wouldn't blow frozen bogeys out of her nose.

Slight pause.

Gideon Well, I don't think so. I'm sorry. And you know what else I think? You're being a tad unreasonable. I've seen your Dad with her. They look good for each other. So my advice: relax. Chill out. Go with the flow.

Continues painting.
Pause.

Suddenly, Kirsty puts on her coat and picks up her bag and torch.

Gideon What you doing?

Kirsty Going.

Gideon Where?

Kirsty Anywhere.

Gideon But . . . you can't just run away.

Kirsty Watch me! You weren't at the party. You didn't see them. Bloody embarrassing. Couldn't bear it! Packed a few things and got out! Bet they haven't even missed me. Should have gone straight away. Not come here.

Gideon Why did you come here?

Kirsty Not to see you, if that's what you're bloody

thinking. I wouldn't want to see you for all the crackers in Karamazoo.

Gideon All the crackers in what?

Kirsty It's what my Dad says. I love you more than all the crackers in Karamazoo! You're Daddy's little Princess! Daddy wouldn't swap you for all the crackers in – Oh, why am I telling you this! You don't bloody care.

She climbs down off the stage and strides through auditorium towards exit.

Gideon You'll freeze out there. You haven't even got any –

Kirsty If you mention thermal knickers again, I'll thump you!

Gideon You . . . you got any money?

Kirsty No.

Gideon Then how you going to –

Kirsty I don't know! All I know is . . . I can't stay here . . . I'm not needed . . . Who'll care? I'll sleep in shop doorways . . . Others do it . . . I don't mind the cold . . . I don't . . . Oh, I don't know!

She has gradually come to a halt and now hovers by exit.

Gideon Before . . . before you go – because I can see you're determined to go, and I wouldn't stop that – but, before you go, will you help me with something.

Slight pause.

Please.

Kirsty . . . What?

Gideon A . . . story. Yes! That's it! Perhaps we could . . . oh, I don't know. Make something up. Like Mum makes up her stories. You know? Kings, Queens, Princes, Princesses. We could do it – the two of us. I know you won't be around to see it when the theatre's finished and everything. You'll be miles away by then. But . . . well, when people ask, 'Why did Kirsty run away?' I can tell them, 'See the play and you'll understand.'

Long pause.

There was once a kingdom called Karamazoo.

Slight pause.

Kirsty . . . What's it like?

Gideon Karamazoo? Oh, it's an amazing place. See for yourself! Look! Fields of flowers. Distant mountains. A river. Cave. And . . . oh, yes, the most perfect butterflies.

Slight pause.
Slowly, Kirsty approaches stage.

Kirsty Don't forget the candles.

Gideon Candles! Of course! Candles! Everywhere.

Kirsty Why?

Gideon Because . . . the Queen has just died. That's it! The kingdom's in mourning. The Queen was so popular. Everyone loved her. And now . . . every place the Queen once visited has been turned into a shrine. Nothing but candles, candles, candles. How does that sound? There are crowds of people outside the Castle. They want some word from the King.

Kirsty He's too upset to speak –

Gideon Said the Princess.

Kirsty is on stage now.

39

Gideon takes torch and bag from her and helps her out of her coat.

Gideon You speak, Princess. Please! Your people need you to speak!

Puts chair in middle of stage.

Get up on the balcony and speak.

Kirsty The balcony?

Gideon Let me help you, Princess.

He helps Kirsty up on chair, then jumps into auditorium and starts cheering.

Gideon The Princess! She's going to speak to us! (*chanting*) Princ-ess! Princ-ess! Princ-ess!

Kirsty All right, all right!

Gideon Princ-ess!

Kirsty Shut up!

Gideon silences.

Kirsty Thank you, people of Karamazoo . . . I can't begin to explain how much your support means to me.

Gideon (*in voice of news reporter*) But tell us, Princess, what did you feel when you first heard the news of Her Majesty's sudden death?

Kirsty It wasn't sudden. She'd been ill for ages. Everyone in . . . in Karamazoo knows that. They sent flowers. So many. But still . . . When she finally died, I didn't believe it.

Gideon Where were you when you heard?

Kirsty I was in bed . . . My Dad woke me. He was crying. He didn't need to tell me what had happened.

Gideon Tell us, Princess, what do you miss most about the Queen?

Slight pause.

Kirsty When she cuddled me she smelt of roses. She bought me earrings. Sad songs made her cry. She always got my jokes. She never complained. Not all the time she was sick. She wore a hat with silk flowers – Oh, I can't do this.

Gideon One more question, Princess!

Kirsty Who are you anyway?

Gideon I'm a journalist from the *Daily Karamazoo*.

Kirsty You must be joking!

Gideon It's just a scuzzy tabloid, Your Highness. Obviously you don't get it in the Castle . . . The rumour is the Queen's last words to you were, 'Look after the King.' Can you confirm this?

Slight pause.

Kirsty . . . How do you know?

Gideon Can you confirm it?

Slight pause.

Kirsty Yes, it's true.

Gideon jumps back on stage.

Gideon And so the Princess looked after the King. Every morning she cooked him breakfast. She walked with him in the gardens of the Castle. She washed his cloak when it got stained with bird droppings. And, at night, as they sat by candlelight, the Princess told the King stories about. . .

Slight pause.

About?

Kirsty . . . My Mum.

Gideon How everyone loved her.

Kirsty That's right.

Gideon How perfect she was.

Kirsty Yes.

Gideon How beautiful.

Kirsty Yes, yes!

Gideon And that's all you keep telling him.

Kirsty Well, it's bloody true.

Gets small, framed photo from her bag.

Look at her!

Shows photo to Gideon.

Tell me I'm wrong! He'll never find anyone to match her.

Gideon You won't let him look!

Kirsty No!

Gideon You keep him all to yourself.

Kirsty No, no!

Gideon You're happy in your own little world. While outside – look around you! Karamazoo is going down the toilet. The people need their King. They're calling for him. Listen.

Jumps down into auditorium and chants.

We want the King! We want the King! We want the King!

Kirsty You're so selfish. My Dad's still in mourning.

Gideon But it's been nearly three years!

Kirsty So what?

Gideon (*in voice of news reporter*) Princess! There's a rumour the King has met someone new. Can you confirm this?

Kirsty . . . No.

Gideon No you can't confirm it or no it's not true?

Kirsty No it's not true.

Gideon The rumour is you were there when it happened.

Slight pause.

Kirsty I don't want to talk about –

Gideon Princess! The *Daily Karamazoo* has drawings done at the scene. These drawings clearly show the King laughing – perhaps even hugging – a woman, and you near by, watching.

Kirsty . . . Fairytale paparazzi!?

Gideon It's best to make a statement now, Princess, before the situation gets out of control.

Pause.

Kirsty Once a week I take Dad to . . . the forest at the back of the Castle.

Gideon Good. Carry on, Princess.

Kirsty We go there to . . . collect wild berries and apples.

Gideon Rumour has it the King holds the basket while you pick the berries and apples. Can you confirm this?

Kirsty It's true.

Slight pause.

On a recent trip . . . It was a hot day . . . Lots of ladybirds
. . . My clothes sticking to me . . . 'Oh, look, Dad! A
squirrel! A red one! How beautiful . . . Where are you?'
Dad's gone. This has never happened before. 'Dad! Dad!'
No sign. Rush to the river! Not there. Rush to the fallen
tree. Not there. Rush to the – Ah! There he is! Wait! He's
. . . he's talking to someone . . .

Gideon Who?

Kirsty Some woman. She's . . . she's charging Dad for an
apple he's eating. Says this part of the forest is hers.

Gideon The drawings show a woman with big breasts.
Can you confirm this?

Kirsty You can land a . . . a dragon on them.

Gideon Bet the King's happy.

Kirsty Haven't seen him this happy since before Mum –
No!

Gideon What?

Kirsty Dad's holding her hand. Squeezing! No! They're
almost hugging – they *are* hugging! 'Stop it! Dad! Come
back to the Castle and – What? You want to go strolling
with her. But you can't – Dad! Don't! Don't!'

Slight pause.

Gideon Tell us, Princess, how often has the King seen this
woman since?

Kirsty Her toothbrush is in the bathroom.

Gideon 'STOP PRESS! KING'S GIRLFRIEND IN TOOTH-
BRUSH IN CASTLE SCANDAL!'

Kirsty She's not his girlfriend.

Gideon Not for much longer, no! Because rumour has it

44

that, tonight, at your birthday party, the King intends to announce he's getting married.

Kirsty I didn't tell you that. How . . . how could you know?

Gideon 'PRINCESS DOES NOT DENY KING TO REMARRY.'

Slowly, Kirsty sits.
Gideon jumps up on stage and turns ghetto blaster on. Dance music starts to play.

Gideon What a rave, eh? No one does it like the royals. Amazing music, eh?

Kirsty The DJ should be shot.

Turns music off.

Gideon Hang on! Don't you touch my . . . Wait! Ain't you the Princess or something?

Kirsty That's right.

Gideon How old are you?

Kirsty Fifteen.

Gideon I'm fifteen and a half.

Turns music back on.

Like my dancing?

Kirsty You look like an apoplectic octopus.

Gideon Thanks! Wow! I'm getting all hot and sweaty. Why don't you get all hot and sweaty too?

Kirsty Because I've got a brain.

Gideon You know what I think?

Kirsty Do tell.

45

Gideon You suffer from . . . bodyphobia. Fear of the body's natural functions. Farting, sweating, burping, sneezing. I bet you don't even enjoy picking your nose, do you?

Kirsty Oh, very clever.

Turns music down a little.

Well, you know what you suffer from. Body*mania*. You enjoy natural functions too much.

Gideon What's wrong with that?

Kirsty It's revolting! I've heard you eat! Made me sick!

Gideon Then try one of these nibbles and show me how a Princess does it.

Offers imaginary plate.

Kirsty What is it?

Gideon Delicious! Eat!

Slight pause.

Go on.

Kirsty eats.

Gideon It's a pickled pigeon's head.

Turns music up and continues dancing.

Look! It's the King! And he's with his new girlfriend. Look at them dance! Go for it, my son! Wow! She can really dance.

Kirsty She's drunk.

Gideon You could do with a glass of something. Help you relax – Hang on! Something's happening. Must be important! Everyone's stopped dancing.

He turns music off.
Kirsty and Gideon stare ahead, listening.

Gideon The King's making an announcement.

Slowly, shock spreads over Kirsty's face.
Gradually, she rises to her feet.
A scream is bubbling up inside her.
Gideon is nodding and smiling, listening intently.
Then –

Kirsty (*screaming*) Noooooo!

Slight pause.
Gideon snatches old newspaper from floor.

Gideon (*as if reading*) Extra! Extra! Read all about it
'PRINCESS PEEVED BY KING'S MARRIAGE PLANS: The
birthday celebrations of the Princess were thrown into
disarray last night when the King, a widower, forty-one,
announced his intention of remarrying. The future new
Queen – an apple-grower, thirty-eight – met the King a few
months ago and, since then, their relationship has
blossomed. A spokesperson for the Palace said, 'I'm sure
all of Karamazoo will rejoice in His Majesty's new found
joy.' Everyone, that is, except the Princess who, upon
hearing the news, packed a laundrybag full of lace
handkerchiefs and tiaras and stormed out of the Castle.
Rumour has it the Princess has not been seen since. One
can only hope that, in such horrible weather, she's packed
some thermal knickers.'

Slight pause.

So . . . where are you going?

Kirsty I don't know.

Gideon It's your story.

Kirsty Then I'm lost.

Slight pause.

Gideon For days the Princess roamed the Kingdom of Karamazoo. She didn't know where she was going. And then, one day, she stumbled on a cave . . .

He rushes behind mantelpiece.
Pause.

Kirsty Oh, come out.

Gideon I can't. I'm the Wizard of the Magic Cave.

Slight pause.
Slowly, Kirsty approaches mantelpiece.

Kirsty So . . . you do wishes, right?

Gideon You're mistaking me for a genie. Wizards do spells.

Kirsty Would you do a spell for me?

Gideon You want the King to stop loving this apple-seller woman, right?

Kirsty How did you know?

Gideon I read the *Daily Zaramazoo*.

Kirsty Can you do it, yes or no?

Gideon Yes! Listen! You must go in search of the . . . the legendary Luminous Butterfly of Karamazoo.

Kirsty The Luminous Butterfly of Karamazoo?

Gideon Sounds good, eh? And, when you find it, you will . . .

Kirsty Yes? Come on.

Gideon . . . You'll get your heart's desire!

Slight pause.

48

*Kirsty looks round stage. Then cups her hand over
one of the painted butterflies.*
Gideon emerges from behind backdrop.

Kirsty Found it!

Gideon Show me.

Kirsty opens her hands.

Gideon That's no Luminous Butterfly.

Kirsty Yes it is.

Gideon It's not.

Kirsty Is!

Gideon Not – Look at it! It's just your common or garden
insect. You think the Wizard would call it legendary if you
could turn round and find one just like that.

Kirsty You get a degree in Luminous Butterflies, or
something?

Gideon No. But I am a Prince.

Kirsty A Prince! Ha!

Gideon Don't 'Ha' me! I told you!

Slight pause.

I suppose you're some kind of Princess.

Kirsty Well . . . yes, actually.

Gideon Prove it.

Kirsty . . . My Dad's a King!

Gideon Fair enough. As for me . . . well, here are my
references.

Takes pieces of paper from back pocket.

49

As you can see . . . rescued this Princess from a Dragon.
She says very nice things. Here: 'Never seen such a cool
hairstyle on a Prince.' Rescued this Princess from a
hundred years' sleep: 'I'm sure he'll look even more
dashing when he grows his goatee.' Rescued this Princess
by kissing her –

Kirsty Oh, so that's what this is all about. You think I'm a
helpless Princess in need of kissing – I mean, rescuing.

Gideon No.

Kirsty Liar!

Snatches papers from Gideon and rips them up.

Gideon Look! You're not the only one with problems.

Kirsty Don't tell me you've got problems.

Gideon Why shouldn't I?

Kirsty What, Mr Relax, Chill Out, Go With The Flow?
Problems? Ha!

Gideon (*suddenly flaring*) Don't bloody 'Ha!' You hear
me? You think I'm just a bloody joke or something? I've
had enough of it. Everybody bloody going 'Ha!' So . . .
just don't 'Ha!', you understand? Just don't 'Ha!' Just . . .
Oh, forget it.

Long pause.

Kirsty . . . I'm sorry.

Gideon Forget it, I said!

Slight pause.

Kirsty You . . . you can tell me.

Gideon What?

Kirsty Your problems.

Gideon As if you're bothered.

Kirsty I am. Please. Tell me.

Slight pause.

Please, Prince. The Princess wants to hear.

Gideon Well . . . it's my Mum –

Kirsty The Queen?

Gideon That's right. The Queen. She's found a new . . . a new . . .

Kirsty Future King?

Gideon Yes. That's it!

Kirsty A King who keeps going 'Ha!'

Gideon And the Queen doesn't stop him. Before . . . the Queen and the Prince, we'd read books and paint and tell stories and talk about . . . oh, amazing things. She wouldn't let anyone go 'Ha!' then. But now –

Kirsty She's fallen in love with the King of Ha!

Gideon The King of Ha! That's good.

Slight pause.

I thought, I'll build this . . .

Indicates backdrop.

She'll see this and . . . oh, I don't know.

Pause.

Kirsty Go to a Wizard?

Gideon . . . What?

Kirsty The Wizard in the Magic Cave? Why don't you go to him?

Gideon I . . . I already did.

Kirsty What did he say?

Gideon . . . He granted me a wish –

Kirsty You mean a spell.

Gideon Silly me.

Kirsty So what did he say? The Wizard. Tell me. Come on.

Gideon He said . . . if I found the Luminous Butterfly –

Kirsty You'd get what your heart desires.

Gideon Word for word.

Kirsty He said the same to me.

Gideon What a small kingdom.

Slight pause.

Well, good luck, Princess.

He strides away.

Kirsty What you doing now?

Gideon I'm going to search for the Luminous Butterfly.

Kirsty But . . . wait!

Gideon stops.

Kirsty Why don't we . . . search for the Luminous Butterfly together?

Gideon You don't look like the kind of person who relishes company.

He walks further away.

Kirsty But I do!

Gideon You do?

Kirsty . . . Yes.

Slight pause.

Do you?

Slight pause.

Gideon Let's start searching!

Kirsty and Gideon walk around stage, looking for butterfly.
  Then –

Gideon (*pointing*) Look at that view.

Kirsty . . . What?

Gideon The field of flowers. Oh, smell the perfume. Roses. And look there! A waterfall! And there – in the river – multicoloured fish . . . What can you see, Princess?

Slight pause.

Kirsty I see . . . birds!

Gideon I see them too.

Kirsty Beautiful long tail feathers. So many colours. Cadmium yellow. Monestial blue. Crimson lake.

Gideon What beautiful things you see, Princess.

Slight pause.

You look cold. Here, wear my cloak to keep you warm.

He gets his discarded baggy jumper and goes to drape it round Kirsty's shoulders.

Gideon Do you want it?

Kirsty Yes.

Gideon drapes jumper round Kirsty's shoulders.
  Slight pause.
  Almost imperceptibly, Gideon picks up torch and turns it on.
  He points at spot of light.

Gideon Look! There! See it?

Kirsty . . . See what?

Gideon The Luminous Butterfly!

He darts spot of light all over the place.

Gideon Look at it go!

Kirsty Catch it!

Gideon runs round stage attempting to catch light.

Kirsty (*laughing*) Go on! That's it! Nearly! Mind the candles! Careful.

Gideon (*laughing*) It's on me! Look! It tickles.

Kirsty Catch it! Catch it!

Gideon Where's it gone now?

Kirsty Behind you.

Gideon (*turning*) Where?

Kirsty Still behind you!

Gideon continues chasing light.
  Much laughter and activity.
  Then Gideon turns light off.

Gideon It's gone.

Kirsty Let me try next time.

Slight pause.

54

Gideon You know, Princess, the Wizard once showed me another way of seeing this landscape. He called the field of flowers a . . . a concrete playground. And the mountains, tower blocks. And the beautiful pond, a dirty canal. And the fish in the pond – what were they? Well, rats, I guess! And, even though it might sound ugly, it wasn't.

Slight pause.

Kirsty And you – a Prince – you could be a caretaker's son.

Gideon And you – a Princess – you could be the most amazing girl on the estate.

Slight pause.
Gideon turns torch back on and points.

Kirsty My turn!

Gideon Go on, then. Catch it!

Kirsty darts round stage, trying to catch spot of light.
Gideon keeps it just out of her grasp.
They are both having a good time now, laughing and giggling.

Gideon It's on the table! Look!

Kirsty creeps up to table.

Gideon Careful! Don't scare it! It's going to fly to the mountains soon.

Kirsty lunges for light.
Gideon moves light away.

Kirsty (*laughing*) Not fair!

Gideon (*laughing*) Told you!

Kirsty (*laughing*) Well, you catch it! You seem to know where it's going!

*Gideon starts dashing all over the place, holding torch
in such a way to keep light just out of his reach.*
 Kirsty laughs more and more at his antics.
 *Gideon jumps off stage, rushes round auditorium,
back on stage, then behind backdrop.*
 *Kirsty, helpless with laughter, gradually gets her
breath back.*

Kirsty You caught it?

Slight pause.

Prince?

Slight pause.

Hello?

She looks behind backdrop.

Where are you?

She goes behind backdrop.

Where you gone? Prince?

*She appears on other side of stage, having walked entire
length of backdrop.*

So . . . is that it? It was all just a game! You've gone and
left me.

Getting tearful now.

You didn't mean any of it?

She weeps.
 Long pause.
 *Suddenly, Gideon bursts in from main entrance at
back of auditorium.*

Gideon (*brightly*) No luck!

Approaching stage.

56

Chased it all the way to the waterfall. Then – Woooshh! Gone!

He jumps up on stage.

Kirsty How did you bloody get back there?

Gideon I know my way round Karamazoo . . .

Slight pause.

Wh . . . what's wrong?

Kirsty I thought you'd . . . you'd . . . Oh, nothing.

Slight pause.

Gideon I wouldn't leave you.

Kirsty . . . You wouldn't?

They stand very close to each other, face to face, almost touching.
Pause.
Gideon is holding torch between them. Now he turns it on.

Gideon We've caught it!

Kirsty The Luminous Butterfly.

Gideon So now . . . the Wizard's spell – it'll start working.

Slight pause.

The King – he'll stop loving that woman.

Slight pause.

He'll be all alone again.

Kirsty He'll have me.

Gideon Of course. It'll be just you and him. That's what you wanted. Right?

Kirsty And what about your Mum? The Queen! She'll stop loving the King of Ha. It'll be just you and her. That's what *you* wanted. Right?

Gideon . . . I asked you first.

Pause.

Well, princess?

Slight pause.

Well?

Slight pause.

Kirsty Come to the party with me.

Gideon Wh . . . what?

Kirsty The party.

Gideon But . . . that's not what I asked. The story. The King, the Queen –

Kirsty Stop all that.

Gideon But . . . I can't just –

Kirsty Don't panic! It's all right! Come on.

Gideon My hair! Rat's tails!

Kirsty No one'll mind.

Gideon My clothes. Hole in T-shirt. Next to you –

Kirsty Stop it! You hear? It's a party. That's all. People from the estate. The same people you're making all this for. So stop talking about them and meet them.

Gideon But they'll just stare at me.

Kirsty Listen! I'm going to have a normal chat with you if it bloody kills me. You remember how it works? I say something, then you say something nice. Ready? Okay. Here goes . . . Oh, I wish I had someone to go to my party with.

Slight pause.

Gideon . . . I'll go.

Kirsty Nearly.

Gideon . . . I want to go.

Kirsty Closer.

Gideon I'd love to go with you.

Kirsty Thank you. I'd love to go with you too. Easy, eh?

Slight pause.

Gideon Hello, Kirsty.

Kirsty Hello, Gideon.

Pause.
Slowly, they lean forward as if to kiss.
Then hesitate . . .

Then lean closer.
Hesitate.

Closer.
Hesitate.

Closer.
Then –

Gideon turns torch off, and –

Gideon Help me blow out the candles.

From either end of the stage, Kirsty and Gideon start blowing out the candles. It has a ceremonial, almost ritualistic feel, as, slowly, they both make their way

towards the centre of the stage.
  Slight pause.

Kirsty You hungry?

Gideon Always starving, me.

Kirsty There's sherry trifle at the party.

Gideon Sherry trifle's amazing.

Kirsty Well, this one's not. Dad's girlfriend – I mean fiancée – made it. Keep your mouth shut, though.

Gideon Don't want to upset her, do we?

Kirsty Guess not.

  They're getting closer and closer.

Gideon Will you dance with me?

Kirsty I'm not very good.

Gideon It's easy. You just relax –

Kirsty Think!

Gideon Buzz!

Kirsty Splat!

Gideon (*with Kirsty laughing*) Dance!

Kirsty (*with Gideon laughing*) Dance!

Gideon Exactly! and you'll know when you're doing it right 'cos it'll be just like –

Kirsty Picking my nose?

Gideon Kissing.

  They're almost together now.
  Just a few more candles.

Blow . . . darkness.
Blow . . . darkness.

Kirsty I think a goatee would suit you.

Gideon I've got the whiskers.

Kirsty Let me feel.

They are face to face.
One candle left.

Gently, Kirsty feels Gideon's face.
Slight pause.

They both pick up remaining candle and hold it between them.

Gideon (*touching his chest*) Boom-diddy, boom-diddy.

Kirsty (*touching her chest*) Boom-diddy, boom-diddy.

They blow out candle.

Blackout.

SPARKLESHARK

For all the Jakes
of the World

'We won't use guns,
we won't use bombs,
we'll use the one thing we've got more of –
that's our minds.'

from 'Mis-shapes' by Pulp

Characters

Jake
Polly
Natasha
Carol
Russell
Buzz
Speed
Shane
Finn

Sparkleshark was first performed at the Royal National Theatre on 15 July 1997 by the Youth Lyric Theatre, Belfast:

Jake Barum Jeffries
Polly Nadine Shaker
Natasha Tara Taylor
Carol Rachel Lyndsay
Russell Robert Davison
Buzz Gordon Barr
Speed John Gibson
Shane Conor Ritchie
Finn Jonathan Haveron

Director Michelle Wiggins
Assistant Director Gordon Barr
Stage Manager Donagh Kerr
Set Construction Jim Carson, David Carson

The rooftop of a tower block in the East End of London. Many TV aerials and satellite dishes, a large puddle, discarded household furniture, piles of rubbish and various scattered detritus.

Some metal steps lead from the main larger area of roof up to a tiny platform. There's a doorway here, leading to the emergency stairs. This is the only entrance to the roof.

It is about 4.30 in the afternoon. Mid-September. The weather is sunny.

Jake enters. He is fourteen years old, slightly built and clutching a satchel. He is wearing a well-worn, but still clean and tidy, school uniform and glasses (the left lens is cracked and the bridge held together by sticky tape). His hair is neatly cut.

Jake makes his way down to main area of roof and sits in an old armchair. He is familiar and comfortable with these surroundings. It's a place he's been many times before – his secret hideaway.

Jake takes notebook from satchel and reads, nodding and murmuring thoughtfully. Then he takes a pen from inside pocket and writes.

Jake Big . . . fish! Bigfish! . . . No, no.

Tears page from notebook, screws it up and throws it aside. Starts pacing the roof and continues to write –

Glitter! Glitterpiranha! . . . No, no.

Polly enters. She is fourteen years old and wearing the

*same school uniform as Jake, although hers is brand
new (and has a skirt instead of trousers). Her hair is
longish, but held primly in place by an elastic band. She
is clutching a tiny tool box.*
     Polly watches Jake from the raised platform.

Jake Shark! Yes! Shark . . . glitter –

*Jake turns and sees Polly. He lets out a yelp of surprise
and drops his notebook. Loose pages flutter
everywhere.*

Polly Oh, I'm sorry.

Jake starts picking up pages.
     Polly climbs down metal steps and starts helping him.

Jake Don't bother.

Polly No bother.

Picks page from puddle.

This one's a bit soggy. Can't quite read –

Jake (*snatching it from her*) Don't! This is . . . it's personal
stuff. You can't just stroll up here and start reading things
willy-nilly! Watch out! You're treading on one now! You
should be in a circus with feet that size. What you doing
here anyway? This is *my* place! Go away!

Pause.

Polly I've only got three things to say to you. One: what
I'm doing up here is none of your business. Two: the roof
is not your private property – unless, of course, you have a
special clause in your rent book, which I doubt. And three:
I find it strange that someone who can write such magical
words has such a spiteful tongue in his head . . . Now, I've
got something I need to do, then I'll be gone. In the
interim, I'd be grateful if you didn't speak to me again.

Goes to satellite dish that's positioned on the edge of the roof. She opens tool box, removes screwdriver and – none too convincingly – starts fiddling.

   Pause.

Jake Is it really magical?

Polly . . . What?

Jake My writing.

Polly Bits.

   Pause.

Jake I . . . I was wondering whose dish that was.

   Pause.

I'm Jake.

Polly I know.

Jake How?

Polly Oh, please – Your eyes! Use them!

   Indicates her school uniform.

Jake You go to my school!

Polly Started last week.

Jake Haven't seen you.

Polly Not surprised. All you do is hide between those two big dustbins at the back of the playground.

Jake I like it there.

Polly But, surely, they're a bit . . . well, smelly?

Jake Don't notice after a few deep breaths.

Finn (*off stage*) AAARGHHNAAAHHH!

Polly leans over ledge.

Polly All right, Finn! Tell me when it gets better.

Finn (*off stage*) AAARGHHNAAAHH!

Polly continues fiddling with satellite dish.

Jake That . . . that voice! I've seen it – I mean, I've seen who it belongs to. He joined my class last week.

Polly That's my baby brother.

Jake Baby! But . . . but he's huge! He grabbed two desks. One in each hand. And lifted them up. Above his head.

Polly I suppose even you would have to notice that.

Jake The teachers want him expelled already. All the boys are scared of him. They call him the Monster –

Polly He's not a monster! Everyone calls him that! Everywhere he goes! But he's not! He's very gentle! Cries easily, if you must know.

Finn (*off stage*) AARGHHNAAAH!

Polly (*calling*) OK, Finn! (*at Jake*) It's getting better.

Jake You understand him?

Polly It might sound like a meaningless groan to you but – believe me – once you grasp the nuances, it's a very subtle form of communication.

Finn (*off stage*) AARRGHHNAAAHHH!

Jake Subtle? That?

Polly Well, he's in a bad mood. Missing his favourite programme. The one with real-life accidents. You know? Housewives setting themselves on fire with dodgy hair-dryers –

74

Finn (*off stage*) AAAH!

Polly All right, Finn! – And everyone watches these programmes because they're supposed to be educational –

Jake But all they really want to see is someone's head getting sliced off by helicopter blades.

Polly Precisely.

Finn (*off stage*) AAAH!

Polly Thanks, Finn! – That's it! He'll quieten now. Picture's perfect. Well, perfect as it'll ever be with this equipment.

Starts packing up tools etc.

Dad got it cheap somewhere. I'm sure there's bits missing. And there was no instruction manual. Haven't a clue what I'm doing really – You know anything about this sort of thing?

Jake All I know for sure is you've got to aim the dish at a satellite up there.

Polly Perhaps I should put it higher – Oh!

Jake What?

Polly A dead bird . . . Poor thing. Only a baby. Must have fallen from one of the nests.

Peers closer at dead bird.

All mauve and scarlet. Little yellow beak. Come and have a look.

Jake . . . Rather not.

Polly Can't hurt you.

Jake Not that . . . I can be seen up there. By people in the football pitch.

Polly There's no one in the football pitch.

Jake But there might be. Any minute now. If he sees me – oh, you won't understand.

Polly Try me.

Pause.

Jake It's Russell –

Polly The turbo-dreambabe?

Jake Turbo *what*?

Polly That's what's written all over the toilets. TICK HERE IF YOU THINK RUSSELL'S A TURBO-DREAMBABE.

Jake Bet the wall's covered.

Polly Everyone loves him –

Jake Love! I'll show you what your precious turbo-whatever has done . . . Come here! Come on!

Polly goes to Jake.

Feel!

Jake points at top of his head.
Gingerly, Polly feels.

Polly Oooo . . .

Jake An elbow did that. (*Rolling trouser leg up*) And here!

Polly Very colourful.

Jake A foot! – And look in my eyes. Does the left one look a little bloodshot?

Polly . . . Yes.

Jake A fist!

Slight pause.

76

Polly The turbo-dreambabe?

Jake Bingo! – Hang on! You ticked! You like him!

Polly I don't know if I *like* him –

Jake You ticked!

Polly Yes, I ticked! The other day he took his shirt off in the playground and – yes, I admit – I felt a tingle.

Jake Animal!

Pause.

Polly I'm sorry you're bullied. Russell is a nasty piece of work. It's like my Mum said about Dad, 'Sometimes the worst presents come in the nicest wrapping paper.'

Slight pause.

Jake Muscles! Who needs 'em? I don't want to do six thousand sit-ups a day. I don't care if I don't make people tingle –

Polly But you do! At least . . . you do me.

Jake . . . How?

Polly Your stories.

Jake How do you know about my stories?

Polly The other day . . . when I was fixing up the satellite dish – totally wrongly, I bet – I noticed . . .

Takes several folded sheets from pocket.

I'm sorry, I'm sorry. I know I shouldn't have. But . . . oh, Jake, there's such wonderful things here. When I read them I . . . I tingle as if a thousand Russells had revealed a thousand six-pack stomachs.

Pause.

77

Jake You see the tower blocks? Over there! I imagine they're mountains! And other blocks – like this one – they can be castles. Or mountains. Depending on the story. And . . . those television aerials. They're a forest. I'm . . . I'm working on this new story. Don't know what it's about yet. But it'll have a dragon in it. A dragon with a head like . . . like a giant piranha. Or shark. And its skin is all shiny. It sparkles –

Polly Like sequins!

Jake Exactly! I'm trying to work out the dragon's name. I was thinking of something like . . . Glittershark.

Polly Not quite right.

Slight pause.

Sharktwinkle!

Jake No.

Natasha enters. She's fifteen years old and, although she's wearing the same school uniform as Polly, her skirt is much shorter, the shirt is bright pink and unbuttoned to reveal some cleavage and her shoes are stilettos. Her make-up is heavy and her hair, though not long, screams for attention. In place of a satchel, she has a handbag covered with gold sequins.
Natasha watches Jake and Polly.

Polly Fishtwinkle – oh, no! That's terrible!

Polly and Jake turn and see Natasha. They let out a yelp of surprise.

Polly Natasha! How did you get up here?

Natasha How did I? – Oh, just my usual after-school abseiling. What d'ya mean, how did I get here, you silly cow? I walked up the bloody stairs. The last two flights need a bloody government health warning. Thought the boys' toilets at school were bad enough.

Takes perfume from handbag and sprays herself.

Polly How did you know I was up here, Natasha?

Natasha Your brother told me – Well, told's a bit of an exaggeration. 'Where's Polly, Finn?' 'Uggghh!' (*pointing up*) 'What? She's in her bedroom?' 'Uggghh!' (*pointing up*) Finally, I work out it's either heaven or the roof.

Takes lipstick and face compact from handbag and starts to retouch make-up.

And, Polly – please don't take this the wrong way – but your brother stinks. The state of his hair should be punishable by law. And as for his breath! Phew! It could strip nail varnish at twenty paces.

Starts to climb down stairs.

Polly What you doing, Natasha?

Natasha Oh, don't start that again! Give us a hand, Pol.

Polly helps Natasha down.

Polly You should wear sensible shoes.

Natasha No girl wears shoes to be sensible.

Polly They wear them to get blisters, do they?

Natasha Beauty knows no pain – Now, Pol, quick. A word –

Natasha pulls Polly to one side.

Looks like we've got a yellow alert situation here.

Polly Yellow alert?

Natasha Don't play dumb, Little Missy. Cast your mind

back. Your first day at school. You're standing alone in the playground. You're close to tears –

Polly I was not!

Natasha Who saved you from total cred oblivion?

Polly You made friends with me, if that's what you mean.

Natasha And you know why? Because under your totally naff surface, I detected the *real* you. The one who, by half-term, with my help and a make-over –

Polly I don't want a make-over –

Natasha Park your lips! What did I tell you on that first day? Be careful who you talk to. Ask me who's in, who's out. Did I say that?

Polly Yes.

Natasha So why the geek?

Polly He's not a geek! He's very nice.

Natasha Orange alert! Niceness has nothing to do with it. It's like saying someone with measles is nice. It don't matter. Geekiness is contagious! Now, let's get away from here pronto –

Polly I like Jake.

Natasha Red alert! Pol, you'll be hiding between the dustbins before the term's out.

Polly I don't care! He's my friend. And if you can't accept that, then . . . well, you're not the deep, warm, sensitive, mature person I thought you were. Someone who's as beautiful inside as she is out.

Pause.

Natasha . . . Hiya, Jake.

Pause.

I'm doing my hair different now. Had it cut since last term.

Polly Don't talk about yourself. Be interested in *him*.

Slight pause.

Natasha So, Jake . . . What do *you* think about my hair?

Polly I didn't mean that!

Natasha Oh, I give up!

Jake Looked better before.

Slight pause.

Your hair. When it was longer. Really suited you.

Polly Jake, I don't think –

Natasha Let him finish.

Slight pause.

Jake Everyday you'd do it slightly different. Sometimes swept this way. Sometimes that. And no matter what style it always looked . . . oh, so perfect. A real work of art. The effort that went into that.

Natasha Hours, believe me.

Jake And you wore hairclips – My favourite! The one with yellow flowers.

Natasha My favourite too, Jake. I've still got it.

Searches in handbag.

Jake But shorter . . . it's like you've lost part of you. Even your make-up looks different.

Polly Stop flirting.

Natasha He ain't flirting. He's talking like one of the girls. What's more, he's the only one who's had the guts to be honest. My hair was better longer –

Finds hairclip.

Jake?

Jake That's the one.

Natasha Won't suit me now.

Slight pause.

You have it, Pol.

Polly . . . Me?

Jake It'd suit you.

Natasha The voice of an expert.

Polly (*taking hairclip*) Tasha, you know I can't . . .

Natasha There's nothing wrong with making the most of yourself, Pol.

Slight pause.

You've got to . . . express yourself now and then. Not bottle everything up. Otherwise . . . you're gonna explode.

Jake It's just a hairclip.

Polly Try telling my dad that.

Natasha Dads! Dads! Dads! What've I told you, Pol? You mustn't let it bother you. Water off a duck's back. Just like mine.

Jake What's wrong with your dad?

Slight pause.

Natasha . . . Hardly says a word to me.

Jake Why?

Natasha Just doesn't . . . like me any more, I guess. If I walk in the room he looks right through me. Or worse – like I've got a dog turd smeared across my forehead. Oh, I know what he's thinking. What he thinks of me – You know, I was in hospital last term. Just before the summer holidays. A whole week. Guess how many times Dad visited . . .

Slight pause.

Spilt milk. Been there. Seen it. Boohooed that!

Carol enters. She is fourteen years old and, although she's wearing her school uniform in the same way as Natasha – short skirt, coloured shirt (lemon), stilettos, gold handbag etc. – she can't quite pull it off. Nothing seems to fit her properly and, even if it did, the awkwardness and self-consciousness would still remain.
  Carol's a little breathless and clings to the rail for support.

Natasha Carol! I thought I told you to wait downstairs, Little Missy.

Carol Didn't say. Wait a million. Years though. Did you? Honestly, Pol, I can put up. With your brother breathing last night's curry. I can even put up with his Richter scale seven farts. But when he starts setting fire to them – well, I'm outa there. What you doing up here anyway? (*She sees Jake.*) Yellow alert! – Geek!

Polly Don't call him that!

Carol Orange alert!

Polly He's my friend!

Carol Red alert!

Natasha And mine!

Pause.
Carol starts to negotiate descending the steps.

Natasha Leave us alone, Carol.

Polly Perhaps we should all go.

Natasha Don't you dare, Polly. I was just beginning to enjoy myself – Carol, sling your bloody hook!

Carol I was your friend first! Before her! Help me down.

Slight pause.

Don't leave me out.

Natasha Clear off!

Carol starts to cry.
Pause.
Jake goes to Carol. He helps her down.

Natasha On your head be it, Jake.

Carol has now reached the roof. She smiles briefly at Jake, then starts strolling round roof.

Natasha The level of conversation's gonna drop faster than Carol's knickers in the boys' toilets.

Carol Why you such a bloody bitch all the time?

Natasha You make me! Bloody following me everywhere. Everything I do, you copy. You bloody wannabe. I buy stilettos, so do you –

Carol You didn't bloody invent stilettos!

Natasha (*indicating handbag*) I buy this. The very next day – Oh, surprise, surprise –

Carol They were in a sale!

Natasha I wear a coloured shirt –

Carol Mine's citrus lemon!

Natasha Because they ran out of frosty pink. You even cut your hair 'cos I did.

Carol I was thinking of this for ages!

Natasha Liar!

Carol is by Polly's satellite dish now.

Polly Mind the dish there, Carol.

Carol Tell me this, Miss All That. If you're so bloody special, why did Shane dump you?

Slight pause.

Natasha Shane didn't dump me.

Polly Who's Shane?

Jake He left school last year. Why did Shane dump you?

Natasha He didn't. I dumped him.

Carol Then why the Richter scale eight boohoos?

Natasha The boohoos weren't for him.

Carol Not what you told me.

Natasha Think I'd tell you the truth, Little Miss Internet?

Jake Why would you dump someone like Shane? He's so . . . you know.

Natasha Oh, yes, I know. Shane the Brooding. Shane the Cool. Shane the Let's-Paint-My-Bedroom-Black. Shane the Let's-Stick-A-Compass-in-My-Palm-Whenever-I'm-Fed-Up. Oh, honestly! Sound like me?

Carol You said you loved it.

Natasha Boyfriend stuff is complicated. You won't understand till you get one.

Carol I've got a boyfriend!

Natasha Tonsil hockey with Russell is not having a boyfriend.

Carol He can't take his eyes off me.

Natasha For chrissakes, Carol, don't you know anything? Listen, if you go to a party, you wanna know what boy fancies you? I mean, really, really fancies you? It's the one *not* looking at you. 'Can't keep his eyes off me!' – Jesus! Shall I tell you what your precious Russell told wonderful, brooding Shane kissing you was? Charity!

Carol Liar!

Natasha Ask him yourself.

Carol I will!

   Leans over edge of roof.

Russell!

Jake Don't!

Natasha She's joking.

Carol (*calling*) Up here! With Natasha!

Jake She's not! He plays down there!

Polly The football pitch!

Carol He's coming!

Polly Hide, Jake.

Carol (*at Natasha*) And he's not alone.

Jake starts looking for a hiding place.

Natasha Buzz and Speed are always with him.

Carol Not just Buzz and Speed.

Natasha . . . Shane?

Carol laughs excitedly.
  Jake is unable to find hiding place.

Polly Behind me! Quick!

Jake gets behind Polly.

Natasha Oh, my God! Polly! It's Shane!

Polly Tasha, we need your help. Quick!

Natasha . . . What?

Polly We need to hide Jake. Russell will –

Jake Kill me!

Natasha (*at Carol*) This is all your bloody fault, Little Missy.

Polly Quick!

Natasha runs to stand beside Polly.

Carol What's going on??

Polly Closer, Tasha – Carol, we need you too. Quick! Or do you want to see Jake hurt?

Carol Hurt . . .? No.

Polly Hurry!

Carol rushes to join Polly and Natasha.
  Jake hides behind them.

Polly Close up, Carol. No gaps!

Russell enters. He is fifteen years old, glossily good-looking, with a defined, hard body, created to flaunt. His school uniform (which would have been the same as Jake's) has been reduced to trousers and shirt, the latter being worn untucked, unbuttoned to reveal chest and with the sleeves rolled up. Instead of shoes, he's wearing trainers.

Russell (*in a voice of a sports commentator*) 'The winner! Russell the Love Muscle adds Gold Medal for Tower Block Climbing to his long list of trophies. Is there any stopping this sex-machine, babe-magnet?' (*Calls down stairs.*) Come on, you two. Hear them panting down there? Pathetic. But, girls, feast your eyes! Am I breathless?

Girls . . . No.

Russell Sweating?

Girls . . . No.

Russell Tired?

Girls . . . No.

Russell Do not adjust your sets, girls. You are witnessing perfection. Look at you! Too dazzled to move. 'The crowd cheers at this spunky, funky, hard-bod hunky. Women are throwing flowers. He blows one a kiss! She faints –'

Buzz and Speed enter. They are fourteen years old and wearing the reduced school uniform favoured by Russell, although their shirts are not unbuttoned. They are both shorter than Russell and, while not unattractive, lack the arrogant dazzle that makes Russell the natural leader.

Both Buzz and Speed are carrying sports bags instead of satchels. (Buzz is carrying an extra one which, presumably, belongs to Russell.) This extra weight has no doubt contributed to their breathless condition.

Russell Talk about fainting! Pathetic or what? Ha!

Buzz He kept pushing me, Russ.

Speed He got in the way, Russ.

Buzz I'm carrying your bag, Russ.

Speed He used it to trip me, Russ.

Russell Out of the way, losers – time to greet the fans.

Jumps to main area of roof.

I know what you're thinking, girls. Why can't my hair shine like his? And as for his eyelashes – they're wasted on a bloke! Don't blame me. I was born with these gifts . . . Others – I worked at!

Lifts shirt to reveal stomach.
Carol lets out an involuntary squeal.

Russell Know what these muscles are called?

Slight pause.

Horny as hell!

Buzz and Speed go to descend the metal stairs.

Russell You two! Jump like me! A man!

Buzz and Speed stand on edge of raised area, psyching themselves to jump. They are teetering on the edge, visibly wary and nervous.

Russell Wotchya, Natasha. All right?

Natasha Fine.

Russell Avoiding us lately?

Natasha Why should I?

Russell Our Shane-boy.

Natasha Ancient history.

Russell Exactly what I just said. When Shane heard what's-her-face call you were up here. 'Come up,' I said. 'Let bygones be bygones. So you split up! No big deal. What's it mean – not twiddling with each other's rude bits any more?' (*at Buzz and Speed*) Jump, you two!

Buzz Stop calling us 'you two'!

Speed We've got names.

Shane enters and, without missing a beat, pushes Buzz and Speed. They fall awkwardly to the lower level.

Polly, Natasha and Carol gasp.
Russell bursts out laughing.

Shane is sixteen years old and wearing black leather trousers, boots, red silk shirt – unbuttoned to reveal a razor-blade necklace – black jacket and sunglasses. His hair is longish and well groomed.

Russell Nice one, Shane!

Buzz Bloody stupid, that!

Speed Could have broken my neck!

Russell Shut up, you two!

Shane sits at top of metal steps.
Pause.

Natasha Hiya, Shane.

Pause.

How's it going?

Pause.

. . . Have a good summer?

Shane still doesn't respond.
Pause.

Carol Russell! When you kissed me. Remember?

Russell No.

Carol Yes, you do.

Russell If you say so.

Carol Natasha said that . . . well, said you said. Said you said to Shane –

Russell Said what, for chrissakes?

Carol Said . . . it was charity.

Buzz and Speed start laughing.

Stop it! Stop it!

Natasha Belt up, you scrotums!

Buzz and Speed stop laughing.

Russell Well, to be honest with you – what's your name again?

Natasha Carol. Her name's Carol.

Russell Well, Carol, it's probably true. But let me explain! I am a dreamboat. You are not. Now, when a dreamboat kisses a dreamboat-challenged person – it's always charity. This ain't a bad thing. I'm giving you something that – in normal circumstances – you wouldn't stand a hope in hell of getting. Don't tell me you didn't like the kiss.

Carol . . . No. I mean, yes!

Russell Would you like another smackeroonie?

Natasha Control yourself. Carol.

Russell Come here.

Polly Don't move.

Carol is whimpering at the back of her throat.

Russell Oh, Carol! My tongue! It'll go deep enough to taste your cornflakes.

Suddenly, Carol can resist no more and rushes at Russell.
Immediately, Buzz and Speed get a glimpse of Jake.

Buzz Geek alert!

Speed Geek alert!

Russell What? Where? – Well, well, well, hiding behind the girls. How pathetic. How . . . one hundred per cent geek!

Carol Where's my kiss?

Russell Get him, you two.

Buzz and Speed go to grab Jake.
Jake runs.
Buzz and Speed chase.

Jake Help!

Polly Leave him!

Natasha Don't, Russ!

Carol Where's my bloody kiss?

Buzz and Speed catch Jake.

Jake Help!

Buzz Kick him, Russ!

Speed Punch him, Russ!

Russell I've got a better idea. Let's dangle him over the edge.

Buzz Wicked!

Speed Awesome!

Jake Polly!

Buzz and Speed take Jake to edge of roof.

Polly He's done nothing to you!

Jake Natasha! Help!

Natasha Stop it, Russ! Stop! Shane – tell him!

Carol My kiss!

Russell Shut up about your bloody kiss! Who'd kiss you anyway? Like dangling your tongue in a dustbin – Right, Shane?

Carol You bloody . . . git! You! You're . . . A liar! You –

Jake Carol!

Carol Let him go!

Russell Hey, Shane! You should see his face! All scared and – He's pulling Buzz's hair! Ha! A geek with cheek!

Speed He's pulling *my* hair!

Buzz I'm Buzz.

Speed I'm Speed.

Russell Don't get touchy now, you two – Lift him!

Jake Nooooo!

Polly Stop!

Carol Stop!

Natasha You're gonna really hurt him.

Russell Trying my best.

Natasha Shane!

Polly But you can't! Please! He . . . he was telling us a story. Wasn't he, Tasha?

Natasha . . . What? Oh . . . yeah! A good story.

Polly We want to know the end.

Russell I hate stories.

Jake Help! Help!

Natasha Shane! Tell him! Please!

Slight pause.

Russell What's it to be, Shane? Dangle or story?

Pause.

Shane . . . Story.

Russell But, Shane –

Natasha You heard!

Slight pause.
Buzz and Speed let go of Jake.
Pause.

Russell So?

Pause.

Polly It . . . It was about this Princess, wasn't it, Jake? Am I right? Yes? This Princess. What happened, Jake?

Slight pause.

That's right! Yes! She lived in a Castle. Well, I suppose all Princesses live in Castles, don't they?

Natasha Wouldn't be seen without one.

Carol No way.

Slight pause.

Polly And this Princess . . . she lived in a Castle with her father.

Natasha The King, right.

Polly Exactly, Natasha! Thank you for reminding me. The Princess lived in a Castle with her father. Who was indeed the King.

Russell Bloody riveting this! – Now, don't tell me. Her mother was, indeed, the Queen.

Polly No. The Princess didn't have a mother. She died –

Russell At childbirth! Boring! – Shane! Let's dangle the geek! He's not even telling it.

Natasha The Queen had been murdered, if you must know.

Pause.

Very nastily.

Slight pause.

Horribly.

Buzz . . . How?

Polly One day . . . the Castle was attacked. By the King's enemies. The kingdom had been at war for a long time.

Speed The King should have been prepared then.

Polly Well . . . yes. He was. Usually. The King was a great soldier.

Buzz So how come the enemy surprised him?

Natasha . . . The baby Princess.

Carol The Castle was celebrating. Right?

Polly Exactly right, Carol. It was the day for celebrating the birth of the Princess! A holiday for everyone. The Castle was full of food and music and flowers.

Buzz A good ol' booze-up.

Speed Peanuts and sausages on sticks.

Carol Everyone strutting their funky stuff.

Natasha And that's when the enemy attacked!

Buzz Bet the Castle was slaughtered.

Polly The King was too good a soldier for that. In fact, the King defeated the enemy that day!

Buzz But the Queen!

Speed What happened to her?

Polly She was shot in the heart with a single arrow.

Pause.

And then . . . her head was chopped off.

Pause.

And then . . . her head was eaten by a hungry pig.

Buzz Wicked!

Speed Awesome.

Carol I feel a bit sick.

Polly After that . . . the King never let his defences down again. Am I getting this right, Jake? The King banned pleasure from the Castle.

Buzz What? No telly?

Russell Wouldn't be telly in those days.

Polly No dancing. No singing. No flowers. Nothing pretty or frivolous at all. He thought these things would turn the Princess weak.

Russell (*to Buzz and Speed*) Like you two!

Polly And, as she had to rule after him one day, and possibly fight many battles, he had to train her to be strong. Right, Jake?

Jake nods and murmurs.
Slight pause.

The King made the Princess wear a simple dress. And only one colour . . . black!

Carol Not even citrus lemon?

Polly No.

Natasha Bet her shoes were sensible too.

Polly Very sensible. And guess what she had to drink . . . Vinegar!

Buzz Disgusting!

Polly And eat . . . Plain bread!

Speed No butter?

Polly No.

Buzz What about margarine?

Polly No! Nothing! The King forbade it! And then, one night . . .

Jake thumps floor.

Polly What? A thump . . .? Yes! That's it! I remember now! The Princess heard something thump against her window.

Buzz What is it?

Polly A bird.

Speed Is it dead?

Polly Its neck's broken.

Carol She buries it!

Polly In a secret corner of the Castle.

Buzz Why do girls bury things?

Speed Instead of cutting them up?

Jake . . . There's something inside the bird.

Polly What, Jake?

Buzz Yeah, what?

Speed What?

Carol What?

Slight pause.

Jake . . . A flower seed.

Polly Of course. The bird's dinner! So, when the bird is buried – the seed grows! And next summer –

Takes hairclip from pocket.

Look! I'm going to wear it in my hair.

Buzz Don't let the King see.

Polly Too late!

Carol Yellow alert.

Polly The Princess says, 'I'm sorry, Dad! Please! It's just a flower. Please – Ahhh!'

Speed What's happened?

Polly He's . . . he's hit me.

Russell Bully!

Pause.

Polly 'What's that, Dad? Oh, no! No!'

Carol What's he say?

Buzz What?

Speed What?

Polly . . . He doesn't want a daughter like me.

Natasha No!

Jake You're banished!

Slight pause.

Polly I leave the Castle.

She walks around roof.

And for a while . . . there's nothing. I don't know where I'm going. Just . . . a wasteland. I walk and walk. And then – yes! – I find a forest!

Jake She plants her flower.

Polly It's full of seeds.

Buries hairclip beneath some rubbish.

Jake And one year later . . .

Polly Hundreds of flowers!

Jake The following year!

Polly Thousands!

Jake The next!

Polly Millions! Look at them! Millions of yellow flowers! As far as the eye can see! So beautiful. And I'm . . . I'm so

99

happy here in the forest of a million yellow flowers. Smell them! And, what's that? There! Look! In the lake!

Points at puddle.

Dolphins! Splashing and playing together. Oh, yes! Oh, yes! Yes!

Pause.

Jake And then, one day, a Prince arrives.

Buzz Me!

Speed No! Me!

Jake The Prince is the most handsome man in all the land.

Russell Someone call my name?

Buzz I said it first.

Speed No! I did!

Russell Shut it, you two!

Jake gets the supermarket trolley and wheels it in front of Russell.

Jake The Prince rode a chariot.

Russell You must be bloody joking!

Jake Said the Prince. Because he was strong and proud. He thought he should walk everywhere. But he also knew that riding in . . . the solid gold chariot was an honour. An honour only given to true heroes.

Slight pause.
Russell gets in supermarket trolley.

Russell Where's my horses then?

Everyone looks at Buzz and Speed.

Buzz No way!

Speed No way!

Russell Shane?

Slight pause.
Shane points at supermarket trolley.
Buzz and Speed grab hold of it.

Russell Gee up, Lightning! Gee up, Ned!

Buzz Hang on a bloody minute! Who's Ned?

Russell You are.

Buzz Oh, no! If he's Lightning, I ain't going to be called Ned. You can stuff that up your –

Jake Thunder!

Slight pause.

Russell Gee up, Thunder and Lightning!

Buzz and Speed pull supermarket trolley.

Russell Faster! Faster! Come on, you two!

Buzz and Speed pull supermarket trolley round and round.

Russell Faster! Faster!

Buzz and Speed pull supermarket trolley faster.

Russell Faster!

Speed That's it! I've had enough!

Jake The horses were exhausted so the Prince – who was as kind and understanding as he was handsome – let them rest by a lake in the middle of a forest.

Slight pause.
Buzz and Speed pull supermarket trolley to puddle.

Polly Who are you?

Speed Lightning!

Russell She's talking to me, you pillock! You're a bloody horse! – Wotchya! I'm a Prince.

Polly Beautiful.

Russell I work out.

Polly Not you. My forest. Look! A million yellow flowers.

Jake But, as far as the Prince was concerned, the Princess was more beautiful than all the flowers put together.

Slight pause.

Polly Why are you looking at me like that?

Russell . . . Like what?

Polly Like there's something you want to say.

Pause.

Oh, I know it's difficult. For a Prince like you, I mean. To say things . . . gentle things. You've had to be strong and brave all your life. As hard as your horny-as-hell stomach. But you can say them to me, you know.

Slight pause.

Do you think I'm beautiful.

Russell . . . Not bad.

Polly Do you want me to leave my forest and live with you in your Castle?

Russell . . . I'm easy.

Slight pause.

All right. Yeah. I wouldn't mind.

Polly But, Prince, my forest is so beautiful. How can I leave it? Even for a Love Muscle like you?

Russell You're . . . you're playing bloody games with me! I never liked you in the first place – Shane!

Polly Don't go!

Jake The Princess could see the Prince was upset. She knew he didn't mean what he was saying –

Russell Bloody do!

Jake So she offered him a challenge.

Slight pause.

Polly Prince! There is . . . something inside me that tingles for you. Honestly. I can't explain it. I'd like to give you a chance – or me a chance.

Russell What?

Polly Find me something more beautiful than a million yellow flowers. If you can do that, I will follow you anywhere.

Jake So the Prince searched.

Slight pause.

The Prince looks!

> *Russell looks at Shane.*
> *Shane nods.*
> *Russell searches roof.*
> *He finds an old shoe and takes it to Polly.*

Polly The most beautiful shoe ever made. Decorated with rubies and diamonds and stitched with gold thread . . . Beautiful. But not beautiful enough.

Slight pause.
  Russell throws shoe aside.
  He searches roof once more.
  He finds an old baseball cap and takes it to Polly.

Russell This is a crown! Right? It's made of platinum. It's decorated with a trillion bloody diamonds. Beautiful or what?

Polly Beautiful. But not beautiful enough.

Russell (*throwing cap aside*) Bloody hell –

Buzz Go to a Witch.

Speed Yeah! Wicked! Ask a Witch.

  All look at Natasha.

Natasha Well, that's bloody typical!

  Slight pause.

Come on, then. What you waiting for?

  Russell goes to Natasha.
  Slight pause.

Natasha Hiya, Prince. So you've got to find –

Russell I haven't told you yet!

Natasha I'm a bloody Witch, dickhead!

  Pause.

So . . . Little Miss Flower Power wants you to find something more beautiful than a million yellow flowers. I can do that. But first . . . you gotta pay.

Russell How much?

Natasha Not money, you turbo-dreambabe. A kiss. A big smakeroo. Mouth open. Tongue in lung.

Russell What? Here? In front of . . . everyone?

Natasha But we're in my own witchy hovel.

Russell looks at Shane, then back at Natasha.

Natasha I'm waiting.

Russell kisses Natasha. It grows increasingly passionate. Carol slaps at Russell.

Carol Stop it! You sod! Why her?

Russell Hey! What's your problem?

Carol It's not fair –

Natasha Calm down! Jesus! Get a grip!

Carol calms.

Natasha You make yourself look a bloody idiot sometimes. Then wonder why everyone's laughing at you. It's humiliating. You should be bloody ashamed. Hear me? Ashamed.

Slight pause.

You'll have to forgive my little creature, Prince.

Russell Little creature?

Natasha . . . My pet frog.

Slight pause.

Carol . . . Croak, croak.

Natasha And now, Prince. I'll grant your wish.

Takes spray from handbag.

This is my most magic potion. One spray of this and the Princess will quiver and swoon.

Russell What you think I am?

Russell turns to face Shane.

Shane?

Natasha sprays perfume on Russell.

Russell Stop!

Natasha Done now!

Buzz and Speed laugh.

Russell It's the knacker's yard for you two!

Pause.

Polly Mmmm . . . what's that smell?

Slight pause.
Russell goes to Polly.

Very, very beautiful. But . . . a bit too fruity for my taste.

Russell That's it! Enough!

Shane You shouldn't have trusted the Witch.

Russell *You* did!

Shane Her magic potion worked then –

Jake Said the Wizard.

Pause.

Shane . . . Let me tell you about the Witch.

Slight pause.

A million years ago I met her. On a planet far away. She was a powerful sorceress then. Her magic potion was the most potent in the universe. Savage monsters could be tamed with one whiff. I was tamed.

Slight pause.

And then, one day, she refused to answer when I called her name. I screamed so loud stars became supernova.

Slight pause.

She has spent a million years avoiding me. Fleeing each planet as I arrive. I never worked out why she loved me so much one day . . . then, the next, not at all.

Slight pause.

An egg.

Natasha Wh . . . what?

Slight pause.

Jake A Dragon's egg.

Polly A Dragon's egg, yes!

Buzz Wicked!

Speed Awesome!

Carol What about it?

Slight pause.

Jake . . . The Wizard told the Prince about this Dragon. It lives in the mountain –

Polly I've heard about this Dragon. It's got jaws like a shark.

Jake And scales like sequins.

Polly And this Dragon – yes, of course! – it lays eggs.

Jake (*with Polly*) Eggs more beautiful than a million yellow flowers!

Polly (*with Jake*) Eggs more beautiful than a million yellow flowers!

Pause.

Shane Go to the mountains. Find the Dragon's egg. The Princess will be yours.

Buzz But . . . won't there be two Dragons.

Speed A Mummy and a Daddy?

Jake It's an hermaphrodite Dragon.

Slight pause.

Half boy, half girl.

Russell Relative of yours, Jake?

Jake It's a ferocious Dragon. It might be covered with sequins. But each sequin is as sharp as a razor blade.

Slight pause.

Be careful, Prince.

Pause.

Russell (*in sports commentator voice*) 'The Prince faces the challenge without fear. Is this the bravest man on earth or what? In a few incredible strides he scales the heights of the mountain.'

Climbs metal stairs.

'It's freezing cold, but is the Prince shivering? No! He's not even wearing protective clothing. Is this man mortal? we have to ask ourselves. And there . . . Is it? Yes! I believe it is! He's found it! Easy!'

Takes football from his sports bag.

The Dragon's egg!

Shane The cold must be making the Prince hallucinate.

Pause.

Russell 'Undeterred, the turbo-dreamboat of a Prince

searches again! What stamina! What grit! And now –
Yes!'

Lifts an old lampshade in air.

The Dragon's egg!

Shane Hallucination.

Russell What then, for chrissakes?

Carol I'll help you! Yeah, me, the frog! You see, ever
since you came to visit the Witch . . . I've been thinking
about you. Richter scale eight crush. Can't help it. Don't
understand it – Before you say anything, I don't want a
kiss. You don't fancy frogs. That's your problem. No
reason to hate you. I'll find a frog of my own to snog
when this is over. In the meantime, there's the egg.

She points.

Russell Where?

Carol There!

Russell But what? Where?

Pause.

Ah! I get it! Hallucination and all that. Imagination. Nice
one. Yeah, yeah . . . Yes! I see it! There! More beautiful
than anything I ever thought I'd find.

Shane Describe it.

Slight pause.

Russell It's in a nest. A huge nest. Trees instead of twigs.
All twisted and broken together. Bushes instead of
leaves . . .

Slight pause.

The egg's in the middle. Very big! Sparkling with a million

colours . . . I'm climbing into the nest now . . . Insects
buzz all round me . . . Wood cracks at my feet . . .

Mimes picking up the egg and descends metal steps.

The Princess will be mine!

Natasha You helped him, you frog!

Carol You made me a frog! With the last Witch I served I
was a cat! A sleek, graceful cat with big green eyes. Yes, I
change depending on who I'm with. But it's the Witch that
changes me. You hear that? I don't change myself. I hate you
for changing me into a frog. I hate you for laughing because
someone . . . someone I love thinks I'm ugly.

Russell I don't think you're ugly.

Carol Then why didn't you kiss me?

Russell Because I don't feel . . . like that towards you.
Doesn't mean I think you're ugly. We can be, you
know . . .

Carol What?

Russell You know.

Carol No. What?

Russell . . . Well, we don't have to be enemies.

Slight pause.

Jake And look! You're not a frog any more. You're a
beautiful nightingale.

Carol A nightingale! – Princess! Look what the Prince has
found!

Russell The Dragon's egg!

Polly Take me to your Castle.

Jake And the Prince and Princess were married!

Polly and Russell parade hand in hand.
Everyone, except Natasha, cheers and claps.
Buzz and Speed tear bits of paper up and throw them as confetti.

Natasha It's not over!

The celebration dies down.

Natasha What? You think it's that bloody easy. Find a beautiful egg and all live happily ever after – You make me puke!

Shane . . . What you going to do?

Slight pause.

Natasha Curse the egg!

Russell What curse?

Natasha The egg's beauty! It'll be too much for the Princess! It'll . . . hypnotize her. Possess her! Yes!

Pause.

Do it!

Slight pause.

Do it!

Slight pause.
Polly sits in armchair and stares in front of her.

Polly Oh, the colours! The lights! The shapes!

Russell goes to Shane.

Russell I've got a feeling that Witch has cursed the egg.

Shane Spot on.

Russell You're a bloody Wizard. Break the spell.

Shane It's too powerful for me.

Russell What now?

Shane Does the Princess love you?

Russell Who knows?

Shane Do you love her?

Russell I . . . well . . .

Shane *Could* you love her?

Russell . . . Probably.

Shane Then you must go to her. Every day. Tell her how much she means to you. Perhaps, in time, she will love you back. Who knows? This love might break the spell.

Russell You don't sound too sure.

Shane I'm not.

Slight pause.
Russell goes to Polly.

Russell Wotchya, Princess. You know, I've been thinking about you . . . a lot. You know? In my mind! You pop into it.

Pause.

I've never spoken to anyone like this before –

Buzz and Speed giggle.

Shut up, you two. This is important. Help or clear off!

Buzz Sorry.

Speed Sorry.

Slight pause.

Russell I've seen lots of nasty things, Princess. In battles. You know? It's hard out there. Tough. I've seen friends really hurt. You know what I'm saying? Out there – I've done what . . . what a Prince had to do. Otherwise . . . well, he'll never be King.

Pause.

Princess . . . please . . . listen to me. I'm trying . . .

Polly Oh, Prince.

Jake It's cracking!

Shane The egg!

Polly It mustn't hatch! No! No!

Polly picks up imaginary egg and starts to run.
    Russell, Buzz and Speed chase after her.
    Everyone is crying out, adding to the general
    pandemonium.

Jake Catch her!

Russell Stop!

Shane Don't panic!

Buzz It's all right!

Speed Don't worry!

Polly The egg mustn't break!

Buzz She's lost it!

Speed Going doolally.

Carol Princess!

Jake Mind the edge!

Polly is standing by her satellite dish now.

Polly I hate you! Hate what you've done to my beautiful egg! You monster! Hate you!

Buzz Who's she talking to?

Speed The baby Dragon.

Carol It's hatched.

Buzz It's at her feet.

Shane She's going to kill it!

Natasha No!

Russell No!

Carol No!

Buzz No!

Speed No!

Natasha rushes to Shane.

Natasha Shane! Don't let her! Please! I never meant this to happen!

Polly screams out and violently stamps her foot.
Silence.
Long pause.

Natasha Wh . . . what have you done?

Slight pause.
Slowly, Natasha goes to Polly.
She sees the dead bird.

Natasha It's dead!

Natasha falls against satellite dish.
Shane rushes to Natasha.

Shane Tasha!

Finn (*off stage*) AHHHHHHHHGHH!

Everyone freezes
Slight pause.

Russell What's that?

Buzz That noise.

Speed I think it's –

Buzz It is!

Russell Can't be!

Carol It is!

Speed (*with Buzz*) Him!

Buzz (*with Speed*) Him!

Russell Run!

Russell, Buzz and Speed explode in activity and scarper for stairs.

Finn enters. He is fifteen years old and very large, in all directions, for his age. He is wearing well-worn black jeans, boots and a T-shirt emblazoned with some heavy-metal logo, many silver rings and studded wristbands. His hair is extremely long and – like the rest of him – in need of a wash.

Finn WAAAAAGOOOOOAAAH!

Russell, Buzz and Speed yelp and scarper.

Russell The Monster!

Buzz The Monster!

Speed The Monster!

Russell, Buzz and Speed hide.

Polly Don't call him that! You'll upset him! – It's all right, Finn.

Finn WAAAAGOOOOOAAAH!

Polly Shhh! Don't worry, Finn. I'll explain.

Polly whispers in Finn's ear.
  She points at Jake.
  Jake gasps.
  Finn murmurs and nods.

Polly continues whispering in Finn's ear.
  She points at Natasha.
  Natasha gasps.
  Finn murmurs and nods.

Polly continues whispering in Finn's ear.
  She points at Carol.
  Carol gasps.
  Finn murmurs and nods.

Polly continues whispering in Finn's ear.
  She points at Russell.
  Russell cries out.
  Finn murmurs and nods.

Polly continues whispering in Finn's ear.
  She points at Buzz and Speed.
  They both yell.
  Finn murmurs and nods.

Polly continues whispering in Finn's ear.
  She points at Shane.
  Finn murmurs and nods.

Polly points at herself.
  Finn's nodding and murmuring get more emphatic.
  Polly points at dead bird.
  Finn's nodding and murmuring get even more emphatic.

Polly points at Finn.
  Finn nods and cries out gleefully and grabs hold of Polly.

Polly The Dragon! Help!

Russell The Dragon?

Buzz Him!

Speed He's the Dragon?

Polly Show them, Finn?

  Finn claws his hands and roars.

Finn RAAAAAGGGHHHHH!

All The Dragon!

Russell He's gonna do it!

Finn RAAAAAGGGHHHHH!

Polly Help! Help! I've killed what was in the egg. Now the Dragon's kidnapped me for revenge. He's taken me to the top of the mountain. Help! Help!

Natasha It's all my fault!

Russell No mine!

Carol No mine!

Jake Mine!

Buzz How's it your fault?

Speed Who are you in all this anyway?

Jake I'm . . . her father.

  Slight pause.

Russell The King!

Carol The one who wouldn't let her grow a flower.

Buzz The one told her to clear off.

Jake That's me!

Speed Then it *is* your fault!

Russell Where you been all this bloody time?

Jake After what I did to my daughter . . . I realized I was wrong. I . . . I was so upset. I hid. Wouldn't show my face. Thought no one would want to see my face anyway. But then . . . then I realized. That wasn't the answer. It just made the problem worse. So now . . . now I'm not hiding any more. I'm here to save my daughter. Save her from the Dragon. Is there anyone brave enough to help me?

Russell I will.

Buzz Me too.

Speed And me.

Natasha And me.

Shane And me.

Carol And me!

Buzz What can you do?

Speed You're a bloody nightingale.

Natasha Not any more she's not! Like the King, I'm sorry for what I've done. I've been a bit of a cow really. Let's be friends again – I make you human!

Buzz What about me?

Speed And me.

Shane You too! Human! Human!

Polly Any chance of a bloody rescue!

Jake Arm yourselves!

They rush around finding dustbin lids and other detritus to use as shields and weapons, etc.
    Jake finds an old umbrella to use as a sword.
    Much noise and activity.
    Jake stands on an old milk crate. The others gather round him and cheer. They continue to cheer at key moments throughout the following speech.

Jake Today we do battle! Battle with a terrible Dragon. A ferocious Dragon. A Dragon with jaws like a shark. A Dragon with scales sharp as razors. A Dragon who glitters bright enough to blind! But a Dragon we must fight! And it's a fight we will win! We'll win because we'll fight it together. Individually – we don't stand a chance. But together – oh, look at us! We are invincible! Are we together?

All Yes!

Jake (*louder*) Are we united?

All (*louder*) Yes!

Jake Then the Dragon is doomed. This Dragon called . . . Sparkleshark!

All (*chanting*) Sparkleshark! Sparkleshark! Sparkleshark! Sparkleshark!

Everything explodes into action.
    The chanting is loud and vigorous.
    Various bits of detritus are used as drums.

Jake, Natasha, Carol, Russell, Buzz, Speed and Shane pursue the fleeing Polly and Finn around the roof.

Polly is screaming.
    Finn is roaring.

The chanting and general clamour get louder and louder.
    Everyone, although taking their various roles very seriously, is thoroughly enjoying themselves.

Buzz, Speed and Carol help each other over various obstacles etc.
    Likewise, Shane helps Natasha, and Russell helps Jake.

Finally, Finn is surrounded.
    He lashes out with his clawed hands.

Polly watches from one side.

Finn RAAAAAGGGHHHHH!!!

Buzz Get him!

Speed Kill him!

Carol Save the Princess!

    Slight pause.
    Tentatively, Russell approaches Finn.

Jake No, Prince! This is my job! I'm the one who started it all. I must be the one to end.

Russell But I'm stronger than you!

Finn RAAAAAGGGHHHHH!!!

Russell (*at Jake*) You're right! You do it!

    Jake – his umbrella raised – approaches Finn.
    Finn is roaring and clawing at him.
    Polly is screaming.
    The others are avidly cheering Jake on.

    Suddenly, Finn lashes out at Jake.
    Jake cries out and falls to the floor.

Russell rushes forward and pulls Jake away from Finn.

Jake Wh . . . what are you doing?

Russell The Dragon's broken your arm. You can't carry on. Let me take your sword. Please.

Jake gives Russell the umbrella.

Jake Thank you, Prince.

Carol Save the Princess!

Buzz Do it, Prince!

Speed Do it!

Natasha Kill the Dragon.

All (*chanting*) Kill! Kill! Kill! Kill! Kill!

Russell approaches Finn.
  They circle each other for a while.
  Everyone cheers, claps, stamps their feet, chants, etc.

Finn is clawing at Russell.
  Russell is swinging the umbrella. They do this in slow motion, playfully exaggerating every sound and gesture.

In the course of the ensuing fight, Russell's umbrella touches Finn's arm.
  Finn lets out a roar.

Then Finn touches Russell's chest.
  Russell lets out a roar.

The crowd continues cheering etc.

Finally, Finn is beaten to the ground.
  Russell raises his umbrella.

All Kill! Kill! Kill! Kill! Kill!

Russell Die, Sparkleshark! Die!

Then just as Russell is about to strike –

Polly STOP!

Polly rushes to Finn and cradles his head in her lap.
Everyone is still and silent.
Pause.

Polly This is a good Dragon! A kind Dragon! Yes, I know it kidnapped me. But look what I did. I destroyed its egg! The egg more beautiful than a million yellow flowers.

Pause.

And while I've been on this mountain the Dragon has looked after me. Kept me warm at night. Given me food. And I've learned to understand what it's saying.

Finn (*softly*) Raaagghhhaaa.

Polly Yes, my kind Dragon. I'll tell them – Everyone is afraid of him because of what he looks like.

Finn (*softly*) Raaaghhhaaa.

Polly At night, the Dragon spreads its magnificent wings and there's no one there to marvel how they sparkle by moonlight.

Finn starts to weep.
Slight pause.

Natasha The Dragon's crying.

Carol Poor Dragon.

Buzz Don't cry.

Speed Don't.

Shane What can we do to stop him crying?

Slight pause.

Polly You must lay your hand oo the Dragon and say . . .
Oh, tell the Dragon you're his friend.

Pause.

Slowly, Natasha approaches Finn.
She kneels beside him.
Lays her hand on him.

Natasha I'm your friend, Sparkleshark.

Slight pause.
Carol approaches Finn.
She kneels beside him.
Lays her hand on him.

Carol I'm your friend, Sparkleshark.

Slight pause.
Buzz approaches Finn.
He kneels beside him.
Lays his hand on him.

Buzz I'm your friend, Sparkleshark.

Slight pause.
Speed approaches Finn.
He kneels beside him.
Lays his hand on him.

Speed I'm your friend, Sparkleshark.

Slight pause.
Shane approaches Finn.
He kneels beside him.
Lays his hand on him.

Shane I'm your friend, Sparkleshark.

Slight pause.

Russell approaches Finn.
He kneels beside him.
Lays his hand on him.

Russell I'm your friend, Sparkleshark.

Slight pause.
Jake approaches Finn.
He kneels beside him.
Lays his hand on him.

Jake I'm your friend, Sparkleshark.

Slight pause.

Finn Raaahhh.

Polly Sparkleshark is your friend too.

Pause.
Jake stands.

Jake And, from that moment on, the land lived in perfect peace. The Prince and Princess lived happily in their Castle. The Wizard and the Witch created planets together. The one-time horses, Thunder and Lightning, became best friends with the one-time frog and nightingale. I – the King – was forgiven. And, at night, if children saw a strange light in the sky, their parents would say, 'Don't worry, my love. That's just moonlight on the Dragon's wings.'

Long, silent pause.
Polly begins to applaud Jake.
Then Russell begins to applaud.
Then all the others join in.
They all cheer and congratulate him.

Jake But it wasn't just me! It was all of us! Together! The story belongs to all of us.

Russell Let's do another one! Jake! Another story! Another story!

Jake I can't! Not now! I've got to get home for tea.

Everyone nods and murmurs assent.
Slight pause.

Russell But . . . we can't just stop there!

Shane We should meet again.

All Yeah.

Russell Next week!

All Yeah!

Buzz Same time!

Speed Same place!

All Yeah!

Natasha And we'll tell another story!

Russell All of us together!

All Yeah!

Russell We should call ourselves something!

Buzz . . . The Storytelling Group!

All Nah.

Speed The S.A.S. Secret Association of Storytellers.

All Nah!

Finn . . . Sparkleshark!

Slight pause.

Polly Yes, Finn! That's it! We'll call ourselves 'Sparkleshark'!

All Yeah! Sparkleshark!

Russell And we'll have a salute! Our secret sign when we meet each other – the Dragon's claw.

Claws his fist as Finn had done.

Jake (*punching air with salute*) Sparkleshark!

All (*punching air with salute*) Sparkleshark!

Slight pause.
They start making their way up the metal staircase to the raised platform.
Jake collects his notebook etc. together. He is the last to climb. Russell helps Jake on to the raised platform.
Slight pause.
They all smile at each other, then look at the roof around them. Then, suddenly and simultaneously, they all punch the air with the clawed salute and –

All (*triumphantly*) SPARKLESHARK!

Blackout.